LANDMARK ARCHITECTURE OF PALM BEACH

THIRD EDITION

BARBARA D. HOFFSTOT

With an Introduction by
Arthur P. Ziegler

ROWMAN & LITTLEFIELD
Lanham • Boulder • New York • London

First Rowman & Littlefield edition published in 2015.
Reprinted by permission of The Walden Trust.

THIRD EDITION
© *Copyright 1991 The Walden Trust*
Library of Congress Catalog Card Number 80-84821
ISBN 0-916670-15-5
1991/5000

REVISED EDITION
© *Copyright 1980 by Mrs. Henry P. Hoffstot*
Library of Congress Catalog Card Number 80-84821
ISBN 0-916668-16-9
1980/3000p.

FIRST EDITION
© *Copyright 1974 by Mrs. Henry P. Hoffstot*
Library of Congress Catalog Card Number 73-9410

Published by Rowman & Littlefield
A wholly owned subsidiary of The Rowman & Littlefield Publishing Group, Inc.
4501 Forbes Boulevard, Suite 200, Lanham, Maryland 20706
www.rowman.com

Unit A, Whitacre Mews, 26-34 Stannary Street, London SE11 4AB

Library of Congress Cataloging-in-Publication Data

Hoffstot, Barbara D.
  Landmark Architecture of Palm Beach, Third Edition / Barbara D. Hoffstot.
    pages cm
  ISBN 978-1-4422-3786-5 (pbk.) — ISBN 978-1-4422-3787-2 (electronic)
    1. Architecture—Florida—Palm Beach—Guidebooks. 2. Palm Beach (Fla.)—
  Buildings, structures, etc. I. Title
    NA735.P35 H64 1991
    720/.9759/32—dc20

91062576

CONTENTS

PROLOGUE

The Preservation Foundation of Palm Beach is proud to assist in the publication of the third edition of *Landmark Architecture of Palm Beach*. No project could be more appropriate for this, the tenth anniversary year of the founding of the Preservation Foundation. We are honored to be part of this labor of love and humbled to realize that in its third decade Barbara Hoffstot's little book is still *the* single best guide for laymen or professionals to the architectural riches of Palm Beach.

Although Mrs. Hoffstot is the first to acknowledge the contributions and assistance of others, it was her unique gift to see Palm Beach as an architectural treasure house and to issue a clarion call in the 1970s for its protection. Many positive developments have resulted from her statement of the need for historic preservation in Palm Beach. To name just two: both the Landmarks Preservation Commission of the Town and the Preservation Foundation of Palm Beach, a charitable membership organization, owe their existence in great part to a growing public perception that the gifts of the past must be saved for future generations.

Through the generosity of hundreds of Palm Beachers, the Preservation Foundation has, in its ten year history, been able to save Palm Beach's oldest house, Sea Gull Cottage, restore the historic Town Hall, create the Earl E. T. Smith Preservation Park, establish a heritage education program for all fourth graders in the town, restore the interior of Southeast Florida's oldest one-room school, and offer a living history program at the Little Red Schoolhouse to county students. Town owned open space has been safeguarded and neighborhood zoning strengthened and upheld through the efforts of preservationists. Facade easement donations protect buildings as well as bring tax savings to owners. Over 2.7 million dollars has gone to purchase property, and into restoration and rehabilitation.

Despite these achievements, preservationists in Palm Beach are still sometimes viewed as special interest fanatics bent on overriding private property rights in order to save some decrepit houses. In truth the preservation movement in Palm Beach has a far broader meaning for the town and its citizens. Preservation of individual landmarks is a goal, but our preservation movement looks beyond historical nostalgia to the preservation of the beauty and character of our town through the strictest application of the landmark and zoning laws of the town. Landmark legislation is an adjunct to the town's zoning code, which has protected Palm Beach from the overdevelopment and commercialization that characterizes some south Florida communities. Preservation, in its most basic sense, seeks to safeguard our neighborhoods and open spaces and the shops and stores that serve our citizens.

How, you ask, can historic preservation do all that? By preservation of our landmarks and the most rigorous exercise of our laws, we can bridle and control the unscrupulous speculator who tears down and subdivides and rebuilds and too often simply walks away leaving a project in bankruptcy. By preserving what is unique and beautiful in the architectural heritage of Palm Beach, the value of surrounding areas is enhanced and maintained.

In the less buoyant economic atmosphere of the 1990s, preservationists must marshal their strength, for every speculator and special interest will plead financial distress for projects that should never be allowed. Bloated tax bills reflecting the social costs of overdevelopment and environmental degradation will threaten family holdings. Speculative demolition of older homes or even extensive estates may seem a quick cure. Preservationists have won respectability, but the challenges of the new decade demand the development of new tools for preservation. Financially burdened owners have pleaded with preservationists to raise funds to buy, restore, and resell threatened property. No such revolving action fund currently exists. Its creation in a destabilized economic situation is a daunting task.

Stronger town ordinances and stronger zoning laws are needed. Our forefathers recognized the power to tax is the power to destroy. Changes in property tax policy should recognize the preservation of landmarks just as tax leniency is granted for conservation of open space. The preservation movement should be viewed in terms of its wider implications in preserving not only individual buildings but also our local control over changes in our community.

Preservation in Palm Beach is a catalyst not for change but for the conservation of our community. Barbara Hoffstot realized that when she first published her book in 1973. It is still true today.

Polly Anne Earl
Executive Director
Preservation Foundation
of Palm Beach

PREFACE TO THE FIRST EDITION

If I had known five years ago what I know now, this book would have never been produced. The road has been rocky, or often lost, and many times I have despaired. But looking back on it all, I have enjoyed the experience and certainly gained a considerable education.

It all began when the Keeper of the National Register of the United States gently prodded the State Preservation Liaison Officer into completing the inventory of the state. In turn, the word came down from the state capitol to the local level to get on with the making of the record of the important buildings in each community. The Palm Beach Historical Society picked up the challenge here and it was decided to make a full survey; to divide it in three parts—

1) the structures significant primarily to Palm Beach

2) the structures significant to the history of the state of Florida

3) the structures of quality and considerable interest to all the people of the United States.

I fancy myself as a professional amateur with the emphasis on the word "amateur." So the first thing I did was to ask for the technical help of an architectural student, now five years later a qualified architect, my colleague Roger Grunke, without whose ability, dedication, patience and sense of humor this survey would not have emerged. Together we looked at every house on every street, and fortunately for us the island of Palm Beach is only thirteen miles long and three quarters of a mile at its widest part.

We found we had to print our own questionnaires. We learned the Town maps were in three different scales and buildings were either non existent or scattered haphazardly on the map. We tried producing our own maps, failed at that, and finally settled for a set of aerial maps. Nor were the Town officials very keen on parting with information to Heaven knows whom for Heaven knows what purpose. In time they came to tolerate us and amusedly look for our appearance on the scene from year to year. Our job could not have been accomplished without the help and kindness and interest of many who work for the Town of Palm Beach. The records of the past have been a real headache to us. By and large, there are no adequate building records prior to 1928; some contractors did put down a certain kind of record, sometimes with the name of the architect but more often the architect's name was omitted.

Since Palm Beach is a resort, its architecture has not been considered seriously by the rest of the country. There is a vast amount of gossip floating around constantly, hard to pin down, practically impossible to verify. It is unfortunate that this book was not prepared at least twenty five years ago as those middle aged persons who originally built the town were the most actively involved and therefore, the most knowledgeable, and they are now dead. The architecture of Palm Beach is, in my opinion, vastly underestimated. I hope that some competent architectural historian will soon turn his attention to Palm Beach. Several fine books could be written here and should be written for the benefit of all Americans.

This book stops approximately at 1945. Hopefully, this will keep me out of trouble with a large group of good, presently living and practicing architects. I have tried to confine myself to the beginnings of Palm Beach architecture followed by the entry of a variety of architectural styles and finally stabilized at the time of World War II. I am painfully aware that I have included errors of my own making for which I apologize at once. I am sure I have missed a fine house or more; I am sure I have chosen some houses with which my reader will quarrel. I defend myself in saying that a judgment can only be selective and personal. I would hope my short survey would spur the professional to write his own scholarly, definitive work.

The words Palm Beach and Mizner seem to go hand in hand. They are constantly used even fifty years later. Yet what has impressed me most of all in turning my eye to each and every structure in Palm Beach is the great variety of architectural design. It isn't just Mizner architecture or romantic looking Spanish houses here. Look around you carefully and I believe you will be charmed. Addison Mizner came first, in 1919, and must be given due recognition for his imagination and innovative qualities. He understood the Times and the Place. He educated his friends who later became his clients. A romantic soul with a sense of humor, neither taking himself or his work or his clients too seriously, he produced an original, beautiful architecture which is still today useful and satisfying to look at.

Palm Beach does not begin and end with Addison Mizner. We who live here and love this island are fortunate that Mizner was followed by the splendid architecture of Marion Wyeth, Howard Major, Maurice Fatio, and John Volk. And from their work, others have come to build and to continue this small town as one of the most elegant, beautiful and architecturally important places in the world. In my opinion, Palm Beach is unique. This concentrated beauty and technical artistry should be recognized and for this reason I have produced this book, or to put it in another way, a more personal way ... to Palm Beach with my love.

Certainly I cannot end without saying a few words in favor of historic preservation. If you like to look at the pictures in this book; if you like to move around Palm

Beach looking at the houses shown in this book, then I think you should give serious thought to their future. Will these buildings finally be levelled to make way for progress in the form of bigger roadways, larger parking lots, and money making enterprises such as shopping malls, pizza parlors, bars, automatic laundries? I think you should also consider your own future and those of your children. Will your life be as interesting, as leisurely, as pleasurable without these buildings ? And will you care very much for your country if it becomes largely one of visual concrete commercialism? The decision lies with each and every one of you, my readers. You will get what you want, what you fight for and what you deserve. So, don't let your very fine past be taken away uncaringly or without your knowledge and consent. Be prepared to fight when necessary!

I am indebted to many people for assistance in the preparation of this book. I particularly wish to express my gratitude to Roger Grunke, who was my colleague in the initial survey of the architecture of Palm Beach. My gratitude also extends to Professor Blair Reeves of the Department of Architecture of the University of Florida, the Honorable James Knott, Mrs. Caroline Taylor, the Palm Beach Historical Society and members of the administration of the town of Palm Beach. I offer appreciative thanks to Barbara Hoff, Ellis Schmidlapp, and Arthur P. Ziegler, Jr., who provided editorial assistance. And to the Keeper of the National Register of the United States, Dr. William Murtagh, a wry salute for having pushed me into this. I can now say to him "Thank you. I've had a good time". Beyond these my thanks go to all those with whom I talked and who gave me so many facts, so much history, such quantities of help and support, and a very good time while I was at work.

B. D. H .
Palm Beach, Florida March, 1973
Pittsburgh, Pa. October, 1973

PREFACE TO THE SECOND EDITION

Six years have gone by since this book was first published, and in that time ten percent of the landmark architecture listed in that edition has been removed from the living to the dead.

At this rate and given enough time and the continued interest of my readers, I may be able to put out a smart new book about Palm Beach architecture and call it *In Memoriam.*

In my first preface, I warned you, my readers, that the life and health of Palm Beach was in your hands. That still remains true. And on the second occasion of the printing of this book, I warn you that Palm Beach is in mortal danger.

The Town Council, in 1978, courageously grasped the nettle, formed a Landmarks Preservation Commission and passed on the nettle to the Commission members. That Commission, during its first year in existence, has authorized a survey of the town which will include, taking photographs, collecting evidence, and laying out a general work load for years to come, and it has tried very hard to inform the public of the value of preservation.

There has been, in less than a year, considerable preservation success but also considerable opposition. Over and over again, the Landmarks Preservation Commission hears the refrain… "It's mine. And I have the right to do with mine as I please." Instead of looking upon the preservation of the fine buildings of the Town as the way to retain their unique beauty and thereby in everyone's interest, these people are determined on their own selfish and personal course. May Heaven deliver us from them, for surely, all of us citizens of the United States would long ago have lost the charm and greatness of our Savannah, New Orleans, Annapolis, Philadelphia —why don't I just say our heritage throughout all the fifty states—had we permitted owners such actions.

My second dedication of this book is to The Town Council of Palm Beach for their farsightedness in wanting to maintain the present unique character of the Town, for their determination to save the fine architecture around us and for their courage to stand up to those few determined wreckers. I am convinced that the majority living in Palm Beach love it and want to retain as much as possible still standing today.

I also dedicate this second edition to the Landmarks Preservation Commission and its staff with the hope that they will succeed in a job they enjoy and believe to be absolutely necessary.

And so, my readers, do you support us? Do you fight on with us?

Barbara D. Hoffstot
Pittsburgh, Pa.
November, 1980

PREFACE TO THE THIRD EDITION

Seventeen years have elapsed since this book was first published. The percentage of lost landmarks is now seventeen percent. This is a significant slowdown, as I had stated in my Preface to the Second Edition, "Six years have gone by since this book was first published, and in that time ten percent of the landmark architecture has been removed from the living to the dead." However, the present trend is to redo, and significant architectural detail can be so changed, mutilated or removed that one can hardly bestow on the present adaptations the name of landmark.

The past decade has been a busy preservation period. Much has occurred and credit must be widely given to many. The beginning was with the Town Council's creation of the Landmark Preservation Commission in 1979. Also, we have seen the birth, struggles and maturity of a private preservation organization, the Preservation Foundation of Palm Beach. And then, perhaps most important of all, the general public and the residents have come to realize that landmark buildings were increasingly endangered and so, the people became more vocal in their defense. Disagreement and dissatisfaction may still remain but that in itself is good for it shows the citizens care and thereby participate.

Almost twenty years ago when I began to compile a record of the fine buildings of the town for the use of the National Register of Historic Places, I was alone in this town in doing anything. I had to go out of the town to ask for assistance. This was given to me by Professor Blair Reeves, the head of the Department of Architecture of the University of Florida at Gainesville. Without his wise review of my work, I would have been lost.

No one had looked at the records in the public repositories; in many cases there were no records. Often the habit was to put down the builder's name rather than the architect since it was the builder applying for the work permit. I can certainly state that the mistakes in my book were my own! I had not a single preservationist with whom to communicate, to share opinions, to receive advice or to be warned of pitfalls. All this has changed for the better. Opinions crackle back and forth among a number of people nowadays. Preservation is fun in this town. We have become a band of Happy Warriors.

I should like to compile my own Roll of Honor to indicate the progress in Palm Beach:

1. I give to Robert Grace the first position. He had the imagination and the drive as a Town Councilman to create the Landmarks Preservation Commission in 1979. It was he who could produce the visibility for the preservation movement here. His services to the commission were invaluable in these early days with quarters, supplies, legal assistance and administration personnel. He was constantly available to the members of the commission in giving us excellent advice and excellent political opinion. He encouraged us always to do more and many a pitfall was avoided by his knowledge of what to do and what not to do.

2. The Town Attorney, Elwyn Middleton, made sure the ordinance was acceptable to the Town Council as well as to the State Historic Preservation Officer in Tallahassee and to the Secretary of the Interior in Washington D.C. It was a neat balancing act. He was patient and wise and

I particularly liked the twinkle in his eye when ever he looked at me. I knew he had my measure.

3. John Randolph, the succeeding Town Attorney, seemed to be catapulted on to the local preservation scene, a scene I would describe as of considerable chaos and ignorance. I believe he arrived at the earnest behest of the Councilmen who had told him to find out what the kids were up to and, For Heaven's Sake, to keep them and the Town Council out of trouble. I didn't think "Skip" knew much about preservation procedures and we had some genial clashes when he told me what had to be done and I told him what the SHPO (the popular name for the State Historic Preservation Officer) and the Secretary of the Interior were telling the Landmarks Preservation Commission had to be done in order to get the Town Ordinance ratified by them. "Skip" was interested in preservation, and, some ten years later I think he is a most influential town preservationist with his legal knowledge and his patient, tactful ways with the Town Council. He was a tower of strength to the Landmarks Preservation Commission.

4. Robert Moore, the Town Building Official, must have seen preservation as a tiny blip among his many complicated duties covering all the daily development work throughout the town. He has always shown an interest in our work in the most unfailing courteous manner. But it is his tact and patience which, I believe, are remarkable. Whenever passionate arguments developed as are inevitable amongst us preservationists, he would defuse them and turn it all into satisfactory compromise.

5. All honor to the Town Council of 1979-1985. Their support in those early days was stout. They accepted every threat and every lawsuit and kept telling the Land Commission to press on with its work.

6. LeBaron S. Willard, Jr., was one of the first Landmarks Preservation Commissioners and served as its Chairman. He then became the first President of the Preservation Foundation of Palm Beach. Therefore he was a bridge between public and private preservation. His organizational skills did much in setting up the Preservation Foundation.

7. I do honor to the late Earl E. T. Smith as a role model and for his work as the Chairman of the Preservation Foundation. The Ambassador—The Mayor—Mr. Palm Beach, Earl was highly visible throughout the town, deeply respected, a true mover and shaker. The town and the Preservation Foundation would not have achieved its present high preservation standards without his persistence and innumerable appearances before the Town Council to plead our cause. We might have finally arrived without him but it would have been longer, harder, more frustrating, more costly, and we would have had fewer fine buildings and properties saved.

8. The Preservation Foundation of Palm Beach came into being for a perceived reason that a private organization was needed in the town. We could operate outside the Sunshine Law as the Town Council and the Landmarks Preservation Commission could not. We could succeed in many instances by, quite literally, not having our cover blown. Preservationists and conservationists should all march together; there are never too many people on the scene to put out a fire. The Preservation Foundation values its connections with the Town Council, appreciating full well that it is the Town Council which has the final say in matters of property. And the Preservation Foundation values its role in educating the public to acceptance of landmarking as a critical one. We look upon ourselves as a constituency, for the more people who support the Preservation Foundation as members, the more successful our cause will be.

The early days were difficult. "What is it that you do? What have you accomplished" we heard often. That was our cross to bear. Ten years later, we point with pride to Sea Gull Cottage, built in 1886 and once the home of Henry Flagler. We say, " There's the oldest house in Palm Beach. We saved it by removing it from the Breakers Hotel property for the cottage row was slated for destruction in order to permit necessary new hotel buildings. We restored it and gave it new life serving the work of the Royal Poinciana Chapel." We can point to the restoration of the exterior of the Town Hall. This now magnificent building is situated on an island in the middle of the main street of the town and is seen daily by all who pass by. The Preservation Foundation raised more than $600,000 for this restoration, and it can only makes us proud to look at it. In turn, the Preservation Foundation could not have accomplished this task without the money and overview of the residents and friends of the town. The Preservation Foundation was a catalyst, good reason for our existence. We point with pride to our present new headquarters across from the Town Hall. Now this is a special and intriguing project. The Preservation Foundation bought an ordinary gas station on a large macadam property, quite ugly in fact. But this was prime property across from the Town Hall in the heart of the Town Square. The Preservation Foundation took possession rather than have the property fall to commercial development. We were able to produce the money no other organization was willing to allocate. The Preservation Foundation then did an attractive adaptive use through our architect, Lindley Hoffman, who had already completed the sensitive restoration of Sea Gull Cottage. With the remainder of the property, which had been the approach to the pumps and maintenance services and the parking, the friends of Earl Smith contributed funds to establish the Earl Smith Park in his honor. The landscape architect was the well known Edward R. Stone, Jr. The lovely park now fronts on the main street of the town to be enjoyed by the public while more of the public drive by on a daily basis.

9. The Garden Club of Palm Beach is 78 years old and continues the tradition of beautifying the town, which was its original reason for coming into being. Their work in the town square area was to create a new triangular area filled with lovely planting in front of the Town Hall and, as I have described before, in the middle of the County Road. This area is also improved by a large standing clock of the old fashioned variety once seen in many American cities and now, unhappily, so often removed. This is a gift from a most generous and civic minded donor. The approach to the Town Hall from the North then is spectacular, a unique approach of real beauty. Once again, this is a fine example of so many people coming together by a desire to embellish the town they love.

I give thanks to all who have worked so hard to keep Palm Beach beautiful, to sustain an environment of quality and to give us all a delightful place in which to live or visit. In my Second Preface, I posed the question " And so, my readers, do you support us? Do you fight on with us?." You have answered positively and magnificently. Now I say to you, my readers, "Don't falter. Keep on fighting."

Barbara D. Hoffstot
Palm Beach, Florida
1990

INTRODUCTION
by
Arthur P. Ziegler, Jr.

Palm Beach is a remarkably small town to be so famous; its population is only a little over nine thousand. Nor is it an old town; the oldest extant building dates from about 1885, and the town itself was not incorporated until after 1900. What has given Palm Beach its fame is the same combination of causes that made Bath famous in the eighteenth century: a very few clear-sighted men—they can be counted on the fingers of one hand, and wealthy families attracted by what these men had to offer; and some remarkable architecture that came into being in consequence.

In 1879 a schooner, the aptly-named *Providencia*, was wrecked off what was then a sandbar inhabited by a few recent settlers, and a good portion of its cargo of coconuts floated ashore. The settlers, hunters and fishermen, who were also farmers in a small way, planted a few in the hope of starting a plantation, and had enormous success, the palms flourished.

In these same years, the seventies, there was a sudden growth of interest in Florida. Edith Wharton, in *The Age of Innocence*, reveals that wealthy New Yorkers were wintering in St. Augustine, in a relatively informal way, in the mid-1870s. Farmers were attracted there by a climate that promised well for crops. And invalids, like these other two groups, were attracted by the benign climate.

1

The early activities—or inactivities—of these groups were leisurely, simple, and casual.

The arrival of Henry M. Flagler, a partner in Standard Oil, marked a new period in Florida history. Originally Flagler had come to the state for the sake of his wife, who was ill. She died, but his pleasure in the state and his active nature led him to wonder how he could develop the resources he saw. First he turned his attention to St. Augustine, and there built two fanciful hotels, the Ponce de Leon (1885) and the Alcazar (1888), and began to make St. Augustine a winter Newport. To make it accessible from the north, he created a new railroad, the Florida East Coast, which extended southward as he developed resort property until eventually it terminated at Key West.

Casting about for a site for a new resort town, he was struck by the palm groves of Palm Beach and bought extensive property there. In 1893 he began construction of the Royal Poinciana, a plain wooden hotel painted yellow with white trim, that was the largest in the world (800 guests at first; ultimately, 1750), and in 1895 began another, The Palm Beach Inn later called the Breakers. Despite their plainness, these were hotels for the very rich, who, in return for fifty dollars a day and up, received superb service; 1,400 employees were in attendance including one waiter for every four diners. Life was very simple: rides, games, boating, conversation. Flagler built the non-denominational Royal Poinciana Chapel for the use of his guests. With the beauty of the island and the excellent climate as selling points backed up by vast hotels, splendid service, and direct rail connections that soon included luxurious through trains from New York, Chicago, Detroit, and Kansas City, and a storage yard for private cars, Palm Beach could hardly fail.

Nevertheless, life was rather routine until in 1898 a new ingredient enlivened the resort: Colonel Edward R. Bradley opened the Palm Beach Club, in reality a gambling casino and the first in the nation to permit women to try their luck. Although gambling was illegal in Florida, Bradley's flourished with high stakes for high society and earned the reputation for the longest illegal run of any such casino in United States history.

Some of those who came regularly to Palm Beach began to want a life more independent from that of the hotels, and so, in the form of late Victorian cottages, residential development began, spawned in part by the hotels themselves. Most were clapboard with gables, turrets, cupolas and lathe turned ornamentation. Their colors imitated those of Flagler's and Bradley's establishments: white, green, yellow.

The Royal Poinciana Hotel survived nearly 40 years. In 1928 a hurricane damaged a portion of the rambling building and that section was replaced by a greenhouse. In 1932 the hotel closed, and all but the north wing was demolished in 1934, which final vestige was spared until 1936. The Breakers burned and was rebuilt twice, in 1903 and 1925, the second time of brick; it survives today in an expanded version as the largest architectural feature in the Palm Beach landscape.

Henry Flagler died in 1913, leaving a chain of hotels and resorts, threaded together by a railroad serving both these and the new citrus plantations that the direct connection with the north had called into being.

In 1917, two men happened to meet who were to introduce the next stage. Paris Singer came to the island under the impression that he was dying. Addison Mizner, without money, without a clear sense of purpose, but extremely talented and full of ideas, arrived with the impression that he, too, was dying. Singer was an amateur architect, and Mizner, a lover of antiquities, was a trained architect, and the two men, having met, began to while away the time with architectural fantasies that, as death seemed to come no closer, ended in a determination to build.

Born near San Francisco in 1872, Addison Mizner led a peripatetic life of adventure, romance, failure, and flashes of success all so intensely lived that by the age of 34 he was seriously ill. When he was 17, his family had relocated to Central America where his father was to be Envoy Extraordinary to five nations. There, under the tutelage of a Guatemalan priest, Mizner is said to have developed his great love for Spanish art and architecture. His formal education was limited: California University would not admit him, so he went to the University of Salamanca, but failed to complete his degree. His family then packed him off to China for a stint. On his return he worked briefly for architect Willis Polk in San Francisco. Overspending his means—a constant problem—Mizner in 1897 became a day laborer in a gold mine in northern California. That experience led him to join his brothers Wilson, William and Edgar in the Klondike rush that year: two years later he returned rich. Soon he was off traveling and buying antiquities in Europe, Latin America, and the South Seas: then he opened an architectural practice in New York, which failed during World War I. He became ill, and a friend raised $12,000 to send him to Palm Beach, where it was expected that he would die in comfort.

There he encountered Paris Singer, the 25th child of Isaac Merrit Singer who made his fortune from the sewing machine. Like Mizner, he was well built, tall and blond, and like Mizner, his life had been widely unconventional.

These two adventurers talked themselves back to health, and began an architectural revolution in Palm Beach.

All the ingredients were right. Singer was listless and needed a fresh grand plan. Mizner had a new Spain before him, one which he could design from the start. He would compress into ten years the architectural history of that country: he would develop the workmen, the crafts, the kilns and the shops that the architecture required. He would have calling at his office all the clients he desired, each with all the money needed to enact his fantasies. The result was that he reigned over his domain as architectural monarch. In the early years Flagler had established the image but Mizner would loosen and enliven it in keeping with the spirit of the 20s, and with a boldness and originality rarely equalled in American town development.

The two men started on a building intended, they said, to be a veteran's hospital, but, failing to attract the disabled soldiers all the way to Palm Beach, they converted it to a club called The Everglades Club.

In design it fulfilled Mizner's avowed architectural ideal which was that a building be "based on Romanesque ruins that had been rebuilt by the triumphant Saracens, added to by a variety of conquerors bringing in new styles from the Gothic to the Baroque; and picturesquely cracked up by everything from battering rams to artillery duels between Wellington and Napoleon's marshals." This building, an incredibly fine fulfillment of his romantic eclecticism, established the architectural format —and himself as master of that format—for a decade . All buildings for any purpose were for lack of a better term, Spanish Revival.

The club also made a monarch of Paris Singer because he owned it outright. Memberships were dispensed almost as royal favors and had to be renewed annually; his reign was as supreme in society as Mizner's was in architecture.

The final assurance that Mizner would succeed came with a commission to do his first house for the leading family of the time, the Stotesburys. He designed a house of 32 rooms, 6 patios, a 40 car garage, and a private zoo spreading over an estate of 42 acres. Everyone in Palm Beach then had to have a Mizner house, and he was deluged with commissions, in spite of the fact that the cost of actually implementing his plans for a single residence could range up to $2,000,000.

Just as the social rooms of the Everglades Club replaced those of The Royal Poinciana and the Breakers, so too did Mizner's Mediterranean supplant the frame Victorian cottage. Mizner produced house after house, sketching plans, elevations, and details at high speed and often without regard to function. In one two story house, he omitted the stairway, which was then appended to the exterior, causing inconvenience to the occupants in the rain. To realize his plans, he set up workshops in West Palm Beach (which, though over six times the size of Palm Beach today, began as a village catering to the service needs of Palm Beach), where roofing tiles, cast-stone detailing, and furniture were made; he supplemented their output with trips to Spain for authentic work. Artists created murals and carvings.

New work was carefully antiqued: stonecarving was chipped, paintings were faded from their original brightness, ceilings were blackened with soot, and furniture was punctured with imitation worm holes.

Perhaps Mizner's most satisfactory creation after the Everglades Club, and still in equally fine condition today, is his assortment of shops and apartments along Worth Avenue, a shopping street of unparalleled elegance. With Singer's money, Mizner bought Joe's Alligator Farm and created a harmonious, delicately scaled, delightfully varied series of buildings, arcades, and walkways that provide for constant exploration and visual satisfaction. His own apartment located on the Via Mizner off Worth Avenue looks out over this splendid thoroughfare.

In the mid-twenties, Florida generally became the scene of a frantic real-estate boom, but Palm Beach was less affected by far than the Miami area, since its character was already established and was thus not as susceptible to land speculation as the less developed areas further south along the coast and inland. The end of the boom, which came suddenly in 1926, may however have had something to do with a change in the architecture of Palm Beach. Addison Mizner and his brother Wilson had been the leading spirits in the promotion of Boca Raton, a resort town to the south which, for sheer dazzle, was far to surpass Palm Beach; it was Boca Raton that,because of fraudulent promotion, figured most conspicuously in the great crash: Wilson Mizner gratuitously announced that General T. Coleman DuPont was a major investor in the project. A news release from the General denying it destroyed the project.

It is possible that Mizner's fantasy architecture seemed symbolic of the commercial fantasies that had created so much seeming wealth in the 20s but had ended in such disappointment. In any case about this time a sudden weariness with the Mediterranean styles appeared, and people began to build in other warm-weather styles such as Bermudian or Louisiana Creole, or indeed to choose much the same sort of Georgian or halftimber architecture that was then popular in the suburbs of the North.

Other architects were moving in on Mizner's territory, the successful ones being those who could work in the Spanish as well as the new styles. Other architects who designed in the new styles included Marion Wyeth, Howard Major, Maurice Fatio, and John Volk.

As a result of Singer's social monopoly, another club, the Bath & Tennis, was launched; its competitive nature was softened by its functioning as a daytime club rather than an evening club like the Everglades. Nonetheless, the architect was not to be Mizner but rather Joseph Urban, the designer for Florenz Ziegfeld. Urban was also to do a fine house nearby, Mar-a-lago, with Marion Wyeth.

Work by all of these architects is illustrated in this book, but like Palm Beach itself, the book is dominated by Addison Mizner. The original architectural idiom established by Flagler has all but vanished now, and contemporary efforts are limited. Palm Beach remains the fantastic creation of one man.

It also remains steadfast. Perhaps no where in the United States has a town held so true to its original intent for so long. Mizner's castles are still inhabited by the great families; Worth Avenue has not suffered invasions of cheap commercialism; the blue ocean rolls onto the relaxing sands at the Bath & Tennis Club; and, surrounded by palms and darkness, the terrace of the Everglades Club is reassuringly illuminated every night, and in that oasis the dancing continues.

This book is a compendium of the extant landmark buildings of Palm Beach described and photographed by a resident who has been active in historic preservation. It does not purport to evaluate, but rather to exhibit the richness and diversity of this extraordinary place. The contemporary is omitted as is customary in such volumes.

With the widespread deterioration and destruction of historic buildings throughout the nation, it is reassuring that Palm Beach, the historical document that it is, remains still so well tended. But "nothing gold can stay" observed Robert Frost. By recording these buildings the author has signalled their importance. That, too, may extend their golden life.

For background information for this essay, I am indebted to Alva Johnston, *The Legendary Mizners* (New York: Farrar, Straus & Young, 1953) and an unpublished thesis by Sally Jo Power, "Palm Beach. Its Life and Architecture (1894-1927)."

Palm Beach Fire Station, North

Sea Gull Cottage

The Breakers

142 Seabreeze Avenue

Mizner Park and County Road

Town Hall

Via Mizner

780 South Ocean Boulevard

Mar-A-Lago

3 South Lake Trail

THE BUILDINGS

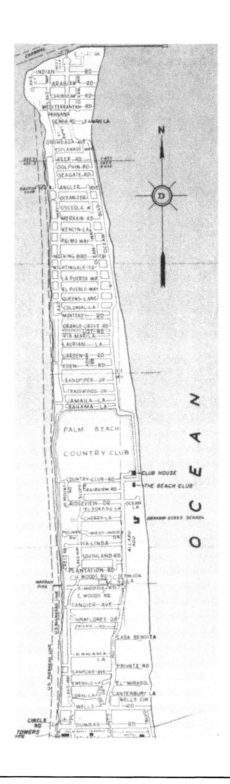

NORTH
OF
DUNBAR ROAD

1565 NORTH OCEAN WAY
Maurice Fatio, architect
1937

This is a Georgian house form built of red brick with wood trim. It has a hipped roof of slate shingles. A most interesting feature is the front entrance. Set within a brick arch are two cypress wood paneled doors with a uniquely patterned fanlight that has a projecting center section.

1545 NORTH OCEAN WAY
Marion S. Wyeth, architect
1930s

This symmetrical one story house of brick has a hipped roof of barrel tile. A feature is the doorway, deeply set in a small gabled portico, and containing a sunburst louvered fanlight. At the entrance there is a podium with a Chinese railing.

1519 NORTH OCEAN WAY
1939

The monochromatic color scheme of the walls and roof emphasize the modern simplicity of this two story house. The wall surfaces are smooth stucco and the low hipped roof is of asphalt shingles. The exterior is simply expressed by the horizontal string of windows, the deep box moulding on the front bay, and the subtly articulated cornice. The bay windows are comprised of fixed vertical panes.

This house has undergone so many extensive renovations that its original architectural features are no longer recognizable.

1498 NORTH OCEAN WAY
Murray Hoffman, architect
1938

An early and tentative application of modern design in Palm Beach, this house has a conventional wood frame structural system but is stylized to imitate the Bauhaus or International Style. It has horizontal grooved wood siding, casement windows including several at corners, and a two story, bowed entranceway. Vestigial forms of the Palm Beach Spanish survive in a stuccoed chimney and an entrance court partially enclosed with a low stuccoed wall.

1102 NORTH OCEAN BOULEVARD
Volk and Maass, architects
1935

This house is Georgian in the grand manner. It has two stories with a gabled portico supported by slender Corinthian columns on tall pedestals. The central hall extends forward under the portico and has a large fan-light door flanked by two Doric columns. An oeil de boeuf window is in the gable. Other details include a belt course above the first floor level and again at chair rail level on the second floor, tall windows of six over nine lights in the main first floor rooms, and Georgian shutters. The house is brick, now painted.

1095 NORTH OCEAN BOULEVARD
Addison Mizner, architect
1923
additions, Maurice Fatio

An exceptionally long passageway the entire depth of the front property leads to the house. The house and entry are of stucco with barrel tile roofs. Here the Spanish Colonial Revival house form is simplified by the development of the International Style. The long central section of the house terminates in projecting two story pavilions, creating a U-shaped volumetric plan. The expansive wall surfaces are unadorned, pierced only by the asymmetrical disposition of the simple rectangular windows and arched doorways. The house served as the winter White House during John F. Kennedy's administration.

NORTH LAKE WAY
PUMPING STATION
John Volk, architect
ca. 1945

Incised horizontal banding and a glass brick window are the only defining elements on the severely flat facade of this Art Moderne building. The vertical panels on the door provide the only contrast to the otherwise pervasive horizontality of the design.

756 NORTH LAKE WAY
Howard Major, architect
1950

An exceptional house in a town of exceptional architecture, this exercise in Oriental design includes a grey tile roof with exposed rafters extending well beyond the walls. Seven bays of sliding glass doors open onto a wooden railed balcony on the first floor, a motif repeated in lesser number on the second. The front door is located toward the north end of the structure.

765 HI-MOUNT ROAD
Maurice Fatio, architect
1936

Unique among Palm Beach homes, this house is built with an octagonal center, and was originally constructed as an artist's studio. The four projecting square elements house a kitchen, bath, and bedrooms. The house retains its original clapboard siding.

700 NORTH LAKE WAY
Maurice Fatio, architect
ca. 1938

This symmetrical house is composed of five balanced sections. There is a central section with three arched openings with louvered doors on the first floor and two French windows with a balcony on the second.

Next are two projecting wings with central bay windows on the first floor and bracketed eaves. Two smaller two story, two bay wings form the final dependencies. The entire house is of brick.

702 NORTH COUNTY ROAD
Maurice Fatio, architect
1936

This Art Deco design won a gold medal at the Paris Expo-
sition in 1936. The house, which is constructed around
an open patio, has recently been extensively reconstructed.

691 NORTH COUNTY ROAD
Maurice Fatio, architect
1930

This two story Tuscan villa is of smooth stucco with stone window mouldings, quoins, and a stucco belt course. The low hipped barrel tile roof has wide eaves with exposed, carved rafters. Both the casement and louvered windows have louvered transoms. The grand entrance consists of a square portico with front and side arches resting on coupled Doric columns. Recessed within the stone arch entrance moulding is a paneled wood double door and a fanlight with iron trim. Several of the ground story windows also display iron grilles but of much simpler design.

MERRILL'S LANDING
334 North Woods Road
Howard Major, architect
1936

Simple frame structures, the dominant form of early Palm Beach buildings, were built again in the 1930s. The center gable and the verandah depict a twentieth century version of the Victorian cottage, so popular in the mid-nineteenth century. The entrance has sidelights and a transom, and there is a small bay window with iron grilles on the front of the house. The second story windows above the verandah are treated as dormers.

246 TANGIER AVENUE
1930s

A restrained tropical classical home with a simple balcony and a balanced facade, this house still has its original vertical wood siding. Rectangular lights around the front door frame give a modest emphasis to the door.

BETHESDA-BY-THE-SEA
549 North Lake Way
1894

This Shingle Style building served as Palm Beach's first church. Parishioners had to approach it by boat because the land on which it stands was originally an island. It has a wood shake gabled roof with exposed rafters projecting under the deep eaves. Walls are covered with cypress shingles and a deep arched verandah runs across the front. There is a Palladian window in the chancel wall. The bell tower is three stories, frame, with a metal filigree numeral clock, and large louvers around the bell area. The last service was held here 12 April 1925. The building is now a private residence.

DUCK'S NEST
561 North Lake Way
1891
additions, Marion S. Wyeth, John Volk

This is the oldest house in Palm Beach in continuous family occupancy. The house was allegedly assembled in two sections in New York and shipped by barge to the site. These are now the two outside gabled sections which are shingled. The central, false, gable was added at a later time. The walls are board and batten, and the porch roof and eaves have barge boards. Further additions include the two story octagonal south wing with scalloped shingles and the glass enclosure of the porch. The house takes its name from a large fresh water lake, now filled in, at the east side of the house where many water birds reportedly once roosted.

473 NORTH COUNTY ROAD
Addison Mizner, architect
1919
additions, Addison Mizner, 1923

The height of this house is unusual for Palm Beach. The slightly tiered low-hipped barrel tile roof enhances the irregularity of the mass and details of the house. Various windows, all of different sizes, and mouldings are randomly distributed across the expansive wall surface. The window grilles, balconies, and lanterns are all painted white, unifying the entire composition. In contrast to the strong rectangularity of the house is the arched entrance, with a deeply recessed doorway.

455 NORTH COUNTY ROAD
Addison Mizner, architect
1919

The rectangular masses of the house are situated around
a center courtyard. Each section has a barrel tile hipped
roof with the exception of the connecting center section
which has a pitched roof. The center section with three fixed
windows and fan lights is a later addition. Originally a road
came across the ocean front and cars drove to the front door
there. The present front door is on the north side on the
courtyard. The ground story windows all have semicircular fanlights, thus continuing the arcade effect of the
courtyard wall. On the upper stories are rectangular casement windows slightly recessed. The house is relatively
free of ornament except for the pilasters and cornice on the
courtyard wall and the brackets under the second floor
balcony.

THE VICARAGE
475 North Lake Trail
1897
alterations, Howard Major, 1929

The Vicarage, a two story house with a chimney at each gable, was built during the first development of Palm Beach. In 1929 it was altered by Howard Major. In its present state, the house has a two story verandah completely enclosed by jalousies and screens. The windows on the side elevations have moveable louvered shutters. Attached to one side of the house is a pergola. In the garden is an enclosed octagonal gazebo of stucco with a bell shaped roof and arch sash windows.Recent restoration has opened a second floor verandah and removed downstairs jalousies.

PALM BEACH FIRE STATION NORTH
300 North County Road
Clark Lawrence, architect
1928
additions, Addison Mizner and Maurice Fatio
restoration, Jeff Falconer & Associates

In the early 1980s the North Fire Station was threatened with demolition; the Palm Beach town council was on the verge of approving construction of a modern replacement when preservationists rallied and presented proof of the structural integrity of the building. The subsequent restoration and rehabilitation of the fire station included additions that preserved the variety of massing and roof lines of the original structure. The original sleeping porch over the engine bay doors, with its balustrade of split spindles, was restored. A more recent picture is in the color section.

44

152 WELLS ROAD
alterations, Addison Mizner,1928
alterations, Maurice Fatio

Originally built as a speculation, this house was extensively altered by Addison Mizner in 1928. The third floor
addition is by Maurice Fatio. Projecting balconies are a
recurring feature. Arched windows and a cast stone door
surround create a decorative front facade.

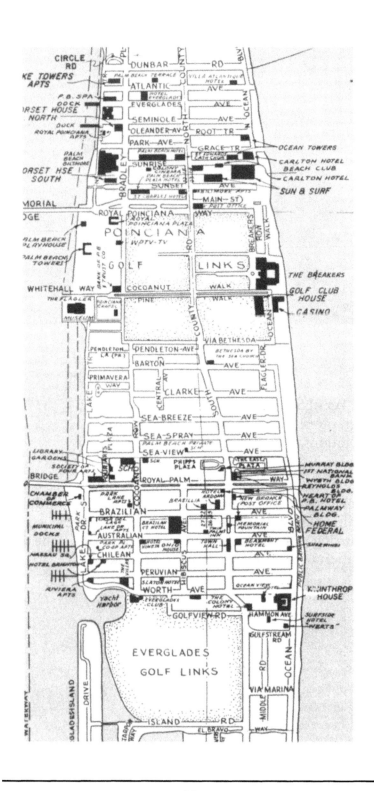

BETWEEN DUNBAR ROAD
AND EL BRAVO WAY

280 NORTH OCEAN BLVD.
Addison Mizner, architect
1923

This house has a very shallow hipped roof of flat red Spanish tiles. It is stucco with molded stucco detailing. The large pointed arch entranceway has a double door below with a pointed arch lunette of radiating ornamental spindles.

110 DUNBAR ROAD
Addison Mizner, architect
1923

The variety of arches and mouldings is the key decorative element of this house. The Moorish window details contribute to the Venetian Gothic appearance. The richly textured stucco walls emphasize the smooth plaster and cast stone detailing.

127 DUNBAR ROAD
1921
additions, Maurice Fatio, 1929

This house is more pure in form than many of the Spanish houses of Palm Beach in that it is centered around a courtyard. The roofs of the main wings at either end are hipped,
and on the first floor level the connecting structure has an
arcaded walkway. Stuccoed walls here are scored to resemble stone. The cloistered walkway has ornamental iron
in its arched openings. The main house is symmetrical, and
on the second floor of each wing a French window opens
onto a small balcony with a high ornamented railing.

136 DUNBAR ROAD
Bruce Kitchell, architect

The varied massing and window designs of this house mark it as predominently Mediterranean Revival in style. Bruce Kitchell's work in Palm Beach is only now being recognized. He was also the architect of two major buildings on County Road.

120 EVERGLADES AVENUE
1910s

A mixture of Mission, Bungaloid and Prairie motifs, this house is typical of the builders' speculative houses built on nearly every street in the early days of the town. Modern real estate speculation has resulted in the demolition of many of these comfortable early homes.

112 SEMINOLE AVENUE
Addison Mizner, architect
1921

The barrel tile hipped roof is prominent on this house which has a bracketed cornice below it. Elaborate Baroque detailing adorns the end window. A Romanesque walkway, echoed by the rows of Romanesque windows on the second floor of the projecting wing, connects the house with an enclosed courtyard. The original front door is Romanesque and is paneled; it has iron bolting and knocker. An exterior spiral stair, a favorite of Mizner's, can be seen in the courtyard. The walls are stucco with cast stone details.

Inside the floors are quarry tile, and cast stone detailing is again abundantly used. There are hand hewn ceiling timbers and paneled doors; in the living room the ceiling— possibly imported—is coffered and gilded. Glass leaded lanterns are used throughout.

151 GRACE TRAIL
Marion S. Wyeth, architect
1924

This two story house of symmetrical design is covered by a hipped barrel tile roof and has a French window with ornamented cast stone balcony over the door, and casement windows. Except for front and side balconies and corbeled rafters under the eaves, the design of the house is simple and straightforward.

135 GRACE TRAIL
Addison Mizner, architect
1922

This two story house has a low-hipped barrel tile roof with carved exposed rafters. The casement windows are unadorned and slightly recessed. In accordance with Spanish architectural custom the entrance is the most elaborate feature, with rectangular and splayed stone voussoirs. The wooden door, recessed within the archway, consists of vertical boards.

SAINT EDWARD'S ROMAN CATHOLIC CHURCH

North County Road
Mortimer D. Metcalfe, architect
1926-27

Distinguished by its cast stone Baroque entranceway and bell tower, this church represents an ecclesiastical adaptation of Palm Beach Spanish. The walls are stucco scored to resemble vertically tooled stone with pointing. Each of the three doorways has a double paneled door and is flanked by Salomonic columns. The interior rises 65'; the nave has coffered and ribbed vaulting and eight painted, gilded, and arched stained glass windows, divided by beige marble pilasters with marble acanthus capitals. All altars and the sanctuary are made of alabaster. Three dark walnut grilles divide the nave from the vestibule; the choir loft over the latter has four Bernini columns. The Parish house is connected to the church by a cloistered walkway and has a cloistered porch surmounted by a balustrade. In the center false Spanish gable is a niche with a statue.

PARAMOUNT THEATRE AND SHOPS
130 North County Road
Joseph Urban, architect
1927

Appropriately, this theatre structure was designed by Joseph Urban, whose primary profession was designing stage sets. Containing various Spanish elements, this creates a rather fantastic theatrical setting for Palm Beach. The structure, with its intricate interplay of geometric forms, voids, and scales consists primarily of a fan-shaped central core with two flat roofed two story wings. The central entranceway has a high gabled roof above a tall pointed arch which has at its base two small Corinthian columns. Within the arch is a wood ceiling with rafters. The remainder of the building consists of various wings, with exposed rafters, fixed sash, lancet windows, and an extensive use of rejas. Important inside were huge murals of sea life extending from floor to ceiling painted on cypress wood by Joseph Urban and removed in a recent conversion.

PALM BEACH HOTEL
235 Sunrise Avenue
Mortimer D. Metcalfe, architect
1925

The central core of this building is defined by the two
bell towers and the central door surmounted by an arch
with stucco decoration and trefoil arches to each side. An
arched open colonnade with Corinthian columns extends
along both wings from the entrance; above them are open
porches with balustrades. The combined uses of smooth
and deeply troweled stucco create a rich and varied surface texture.

184 SUNSET AVENUE
Bruce Kitchell, architect
1924

The open staircase and balcony projections create an irregularly shaped courtyard. Lathe-turned wooden columns and plaster Corinthian columns and pilasters decorate the balconies, arcades, and arched entrances. The balconies have simple cast iron balustrades and brackets. Richly textured stucco faces the entire structure.

BRADLEY HOUSE
280 Sunset Avenue
Martin Luther Hampton, architect
1920s?

Occupying a corner location, Bradley House, a mixed commercial-residential building, exhibits a welter of Mediterranean Revival details. Its charming courtyard is organized around a central fountain. The arched interior arcade is surmounted by a balustrade of tiles and two flanking exterior staircases.

NORTHWEST COMMERCIAL CORNER
122 North County Road
Bruce Kitchell, architect
1929

A blind arcade of pointed cinquefoil arches dominates the ground story of this building while corbels, sawtooth patterns, and dentils stand out above. The arcade was originally glazed with fixed glass panes.

BREAKERS HOTEL
South County Road
Schulze and Weaver, architects
1926

A very grand Flagler hotel, the third on the site, the Breakers was designed by the New York firm that did the Waldorf-Astoria and the Los Angeles Biltmore. The first Palm Beach Inn was built in 1895 and enlarged into the Breakers Hotel in 1901. It burned in 1903 and was immediately rebuilt. The second Breakers burned in 1925 and again was rebuilt.

The present structure has an H-shaped plan with twin towers, each between the center section and the side wings. The two-tiered towers have columns and open arches similar to the arcaded entrance. The different orders of classical columns and pilasters on the ground story loggias, the porte-cochere, and the upper stories, are the dominant architectural motifs. The extensive use of balustrades, urns and relief panels further enhance the exterior formality of the structure. On the interior the lobby runs the entire length of the center section and on the ocean side opens onto a courtyard through seven arched pairs of French doors. This same design is reflected on the ballroom on the opposite side. The courtyard is paved and has decorative fountains and a sunken garden.

A three tiered fountain with elaborate sculpture accents the entrance approach to the hotel.

Despite a few alterations and extensions the hotel retains the exterior Italianate splendor of its first days.

ROYAL POINCIANA HOTEL
GREEN HOUSE
5 Cocoanut Row
McDonald and McGuire, builders
1896

The greenhouse cupola is the only surviving part of H. M.
Flagler's Royal Poinciana Hotel. The corners of the tower
are emphasized by simple pilasters.

The greenhouse has been the victim of ruthless modern-
ization. Its lower parts bear no resemblance to the former structure.

THE FLAGLER MUSEUM,
formerly WHITEHALL
Whitehall Way
Carrere and Hastings, architects
1901

Flagler's own house is essentially a Southern plantation form translated in the nineteenth century Beaux-Arts style. At each gable are twin chimneys attached by a gable curtain. The lavishly ornate verandah stretches across the entire front of the main house. There are wings on either side. The elaborate ironwork entrance and balconies are dominated by the Renaissance columns, pilasters, brackets, coffered ceiling and cornice. Ornate lamps, urns, and plant cylinders enhance the strict formality of the structure. The rear of the house is more simply expressed, a late Victorian idiosyncrasy. The windows are recessed with simple mouldings; the heavy columns have unique structural bracket capitals.

SEA GULL COTTAGE
58 Cocoanut Row
1886

Sea Gull Cottage is Palm Beach's oldest extant house. It was constructed, at a cost of $10,000 for land and $30,000 for the house, as a vacation home for R. R. McCormick, a retired Denver entrepreneur. It was widely known as the first grand house on Lake Worth. Recollections of the 1880s mentioned its Georgia marble floors, stained glass windows, and grand mahogany staircase with Eastlake detailing, constructed according to local tradition of timbers rescued from a shipwreck. It originally featured a three-story stair tower, since demolished.

The house frame is constructed of insect resistant Dade County pine with fish scale shingles for cladding. The Shingle-Queen Anne Style treatment, common in the United States in the 1880s, is enhanced by a broad porch with a Chippendale-influenced balustrade, dormer windows, and a bay window on the side facade.

In 1893, the McCormick house and extensive property were purchased by Henry Flagler for $75,000 and became Flagler's first winter residence in Palm Beach. Around 1913, the cottage was moved from its original lakefront site to the ocean, where it acquired its distinctive name and became part of the Breakers Hotel complex as a rental cottage.

In 1984 the Preservation Foundation saved the cottage from demolition by moving it again to a lakefront location donated by the Royal Poinciana Chapel. To accomplish the move, the cottage had to be cut in half. It was extensively restored by the Preservation Foundation and today serves as the parish house of the Royal Poinciana Chapel and the library and boardroom of the Preservation Foundation. It is shown here before restoration. A recent photograph appears in the color section.

ROYAL POINCIANA CHAPEL
60 Cocoanut Row
1896

Flagler had this non-denominational chapel built for his guests. It is one of the oldest structures in Palm Beach. The church was originally built on Whitehall Way but in 1972 the building was moved to Coconut Row. Prior to its relocation, the chapel had a cruciform plan with an entrance tower. The verandah on either side of the tower is classical with Doric columns, a simple entablature and a balustrade. A balustrade with urns crowns the top. The building displayed Georgian arched windows, a pedimented entrance, and was sheathed with clapboards. Some of these features remain but note the two photographs carefully as considerable changes have been made to the front of the old structure.

3 SOUTH LAKE TRAIL
1891

This two story frame structure with a pitched roof is one of the earliest houses built in Palm Beach, and therefore falls into the category of important houses worthy of preservation. The variety of vertical, horizontal and shingle sidings were late nineteenth century conventions. The shutters and several windows are louvered. The verandah has slender posts with solid bracket capitals.

115 SOUTH OCEAN DRIVE
Marion S. Wyeth, architect
1924

The house is built around a central courtyard in accordance with Mediterranean traditions. However in this case the courtyard was later enclosed and the front arcade has been screened and glazed. The classical characteristics dominate the symmetrical house plan. Below the closed arcade is the balustrade from the former courtyard. The entrance consists of three-quarter columns that support a full entablature, and the ground story windows have boldly projecting lintels with supporting brackets.

124 VIA BETHESDA
Howard Major, architect
1930

This house is a severe Louis XVI design executed in cut coral stone. The very low hipped roof is of flat terra cotta tiles. The coral blocks are laid in regular courses, each course terminating in a rusticated quoin with larger blocks forming a base for the upper courses. A belt course separates the first and second floors. Above the windows are flat lintels with splayed voussoirs on the ground story and keystones on the second story. The casement windows and the French doors all have louvered shutters. The entry which protrudes around the double door is adorned with a festoon on the lintel. Above the door is an elaborate glazed and iron transom. A granite Belgian block motorway extends to the walls of the house.

130 BARTON AVENUE
Hoppin and Cohn, architects
1919

Numerous classical details adorn the house. Th entrance elevation consists of Doric columns, an entablature with a center console, and a lintel with pineapple sculptures. Above is a Palladian window and a cartouche with festoons. On either side of the festoons is an *oeil de boeuf*. The ground story French doors have pedimented lintels, transoms, and iron balustrades. The entrance to the property consists of piers, also with pineapple sculptures and an elaborate iron gate with a lantern.

THE RECTORY
BETHESDA-BY-THE-SEA
165 Barton Avenue
Marion S. Wyeth, architect
1924

In the Spanish tradition, the rectory is built around a courtyard which has a fountain of Spanish tile. The textured stucco surface emphasizes the stucco arch and columned entrance. The entry is elaborated by the iron lantern, the rope moulding, the heraldic motifs and the large, fanciful pediment.

CHURCH OF BETHESDA-BY-THE-SEA
141 South County Road
Hiss and Weeks, architects
1927
addition, Marion S. Wyeth, 1931

The Church of Bethesda-by-the-Sea was built during the late Gothic Revival period that developed in the late nineteenth and early twentieth centuries.

The church has a nave and side aisles and is built of coursed ashlar with a bell tower over the entrance. The church incorporates lancet and equilateral arches, simple Romanesque buttresses and a conservative amount of sculpture.

250 BARTON AVENUE
Volk and Maass, architects
1931

The front surface of this house is a series of slightly projecting sections. The windows on the center section are asymmetrically disposed, probably to accommodate the interior stair case. The window above the lantern is stained glass. The second story windows on the front end sections have hand painted Norwegian solid shutters. The ground story arch windows are continued on the ground story wing where they are separated by small Corinthian columns and display an intricate iron grille pattern. Simpler iron work occurs on the ground story center window grilles, the balcony balustrade and entrance lantern. The elaborate entrance with pilasters, heavily carved brackets, and lintels is pink marble.

150 SOUTH OCEAN BOULEVARD

Addison Mizner, architect
1923
additions, Joseph Urban, 1926
alterations, Maurice Fatio, 1935

The richly textured stucco surfaces enhance the smooth sculptural classical elements that adorn the windows and entrance. At the entrance are engaged Corinthian columns on pedestals and a full entablature that projects to form a balcony. Flanking the balcony are armored figures. An iron grille follows the profile of the entrance arch. A simpler version of the entrance motif is repeated on the ground story window frames. Engaged Corinthian columns and colonnettes occur between the groups of arched windows throughout the house. On the second story there is an iron balcony and an ornate heraldic wall sculpture at one end and a porch with wood reja at the other end.

172 SOUTH OCEAN BOULEVARD
Marion S. Wyeth, architect
1926
addition, Maurice Fatio, 1929

The entrance to this house has a massive cast stone broken arch pediment, urn, and cartouche all in the Spanish Baroque tradition. Within this frame is an elaborate wood
paneled double door with an elaborate semi-circular iron
grille above. The broken pediment motif is repeated on one
of the side windows. The other windows are either casement, or arched with cast stone pilasters or in the form of
French doors with transoms.

190 SOUTH OCEAN BOULEVARD
Volk and Maass, architects
1931

Except for the few classical features this Mediterranean house design reflects the simplicity of early twentieth century modern architecture. The quoins on the ground story and the balcony and loggia on the second floor are classical derivatives, but the smooth wall surfaces, the unadorned windows, and the single large arch window reveal the influence of the modern European style. The barrel tile hipped roof with carved exposed rafters retains its common form.

113 CLARKE AVENUE
ca. 1920

Prairie and Bungaloid influences are strong in this simple but well preserved early cottage. The banded windows and wide roof overlay provide a horizontal emphasis. Several compositional motifs recall the Prairie houses of Frank Lloyd Wright.

150 CLARKE AVENUE
Howard Major, architect
1934

This British Colonial design by Howard Major shows a restrained use of detail. Quoining defines the corners. The use of keystones enlivens the windows and round arched doorway.

116 SEABREEZE AVENUE
ca. 1932
remodeling, John Volk,

This volumetric composition recalls earlier nineteenth century domestic architectural styles. The massing and subtle details create an interesting composition from a relatively simple house. The dominant characteristics are the numerous projections in the forms of side wings, the entrance porch, the second story bays, the dormer, and the overhang roofs with wide eaves. The house is sheathed in shingles which along the rake of the front gable are laid at an angle. The flat arch motif was utilized for the windows on the wing near the street and for the porch arches.

140 SEABREEZE AVENUE
1925

All of the lavish stylistic ornament commonly found on the larger Palm Beach houses adorns this much smaller structure. The spacious variations created by the projecting vestibule and the taller two bay section add variety to the traditional five bay house form. All of the windows and the door are round arch in form but on the ground story they are set within ornate stucco mouldings with spiral engaged columns and classical floral patterns. The upper section of the arch windows are divided vertically into three and four sections. On the second story the arch windows vary in height size and form. The end windows open onto balconies at different heights that have iron balustrades which balloon outward. The house has an almost mid-Victorian quality.

142 SEABREEZE AVENUE
E. U. Roddy, builder
Early Twentieth Century

The screened front verandah and overhanging roofs make this house particularly well suited to the climate. The simple articulation of gables, the frame members, the sills and the smooth stucco surfaces approach the simplicity of early twentieth century modern architecture while the shingles recall the nineteenth century Shingle Style. A house such as this could be found in any small town of the period.

218 SEABREEZE AVENUE
1919

The porte-cochere and a back wing, both in the Mission style, are probably additions to this simple house form. The house is basically an early modern form with deep eaves and simple mouldings.

357 SEABREEZE AVENUE
Early Twentieth Century

The Western Stick Style, a nineteenth century house form, remained popular well into the twentieth century. Bold projections and structural emphasis were dominant characteristics of the style. The steeply pitched roof exposes the rafters and brackets and at the gable ends, the awning frame members are clearly visible. The house is sheathed in wooden shingles. The upper sashes of the windows are divided into slender vertical panes. The height and solidity of the house are contrasted by the low, broad screened porch. Like the house its rafters and columns reveal its structural system.

403 SEABREEZE AVENUE
1920s

Throughout the country the bungalow was one of the more popular styles during the first and second decades of the twentieth century. Here it is well adapted to the Florida climate. The true bungalow is only one story but variations such as this one and a half story house were frequent. In the bungaloid tradition it has the dominant front gable, overhanging roofs with wide eaves, and rubble masonry half piers on the ground story.

232 COCOANUT ROW
1924

The hipped gable roofs of asbestos asphalt tile, dominate the silhouette of this house. On the taller portion of the house, the dormers on the north and south elevations run the full length of the roof. The gables are framed in wood with projecting rafters on the wide eaves. The walls are of smooth stucco. On the gable end of the lower house section is a large arch window. The cantilevered pergola that extends from the arched porch adheres to the prevailing Mediterranean taste.

137 SEASPRAY AVENUE
Theodore Rowley, architect
1924

The Romantic eclecticism of Palm Beach absorbed the Mediterranean styles in varying degrees. Here Moorish North African elements are the dominant features. Built around a courtyard the house incorporates a dome, a minaret-style chimney, a canvas canopied entrance, pointed arches, twisted columns and iron window grilles. There is a large wood bay with intricate wood patterns. The greater proportion of wall area to window space was a climatic necessity in the hot, dry Mediterranean regions.

225 SEASPRAY AVENUE
ca. 1920

This house is a wonderful example of one of Palm Beach's fastest disappearing styles, the Bungalow. The tapered square piers, open porch, and one and one half story construction are typical of the style. The predominant curved rafter ends add an Oriental flavor to the design. This house has lost its original tin roof.

230 SOUTH OCEAN BOULEVARD
Early Twentieth Century

This Shingle Style house has a classical verandah and balustrade. Characteristics of this style are the broad, hipped roof with a single dormer and the wood shingle siding on the house. The roof is asphalt shingle. The door has single pane sidelights, and the tripartite fenestration is repeated in the windows directly above. The other windows are in a double or triple disposition.

NORTHWEST COMMERCIAL CORNER

230-234 South County Road
Addison Mizner, architect
1920s, No. 234: 1929

The scale and diverse materials of these three buildings create a well-proportioned composition. The outer buildings are stucco with cut coral stone trim. In strong contrast is the center brick structure with a tapestry brick-work fascia and a saw-tooth cornice. Various designs of ironwork appear on all the buildings as balustrades, brackets, and window crestings. Individual features include a spiral staircase on the south side of the corner building, a motor entry between the corner and center buildings, and a classical ground story, with engaged Doric columns, on the third building.

256 SOUTH OCEAN BOULEVARD
Volk and Maass, 1928

The lavish entranceway and the ground story windows are derivatives from Spanish Gothic and Spanish Renaissance motifs. The fixed pane windows are recessed in basket handle arches and separated by engaged columns. The rectangular picture window has an ornately patterned lintel with a coat of arms. Above this wall is a Renaissance balustrade. The grand entrance is stucco and cast stone.

FIRST NATIONAL BANK
255 South County Road
Maurice Fatio, architect
1927
additions, John Volk, 1930s-1970s

Bold Italian Mannerist and Spanish Renaissance details accent this commercial building. The elaborate iron grille-work door is set within a heavily rusticated arch with a broken arch pediment. A shield ornament crowns the over-scaled keystone. The rustication is repeated by the quoins. The building incorporates a variety of materials; the balconies and pilasters are stucco, the grilles are iron, the fascia is wood, and the cornice is stone.

SOUTHEAST COMMERCIAL CORNER
239-247 South County Road
Maurice Fatio, architect
1928

This diversified Gothic and Renaissance composition is harmonized by the evenly pitched red barrel tile roofs and by the common use of materials. The buildings are stucco with cut coral stone mouldings, cornices, belt courses, and quoins.

SOUTHWEST COMMERCIAL BLOCK
240-246 South County Road
Addison Mizner, architect
1924

This simple structure incorporates a variety of architectural styles. The entrance is classical with engaged Doric columns and a pediment entirely executed in cut coral stone. The unusual features are the flat-topped triangular window arcade, the irregular profile arches above the second story windows, and the diamond pattern balustrades. The gable end spiral staircase was a modern feature influenced by the International Style; note the profile of the steps incised along the stairwall.

209 PHIPPS PLAZA
Marion S. Wyeth, architect
1925

This eclectic Mediterranean Georgian house extends to the curb line and has both public and private entrance courts facing Phipps Plaza. The polygonal entrance displays a simplified classical cornice, mouldings and a splayed keystone. The glazing bars of the fanlight and the gate are both elaborate cast iron designs, completing the entrance composition.

215 PHIPPS PLAZA
Belford Shoumate, architect
1946

This simple apartment structure has a hipped roof of Bermuda tile with exposed rafters. The rectangular windows are slightly recessed and unadorned. The units have individual balconies and gardens. An exterior spiral staircase ascends from the ground to the third story.

222 PHIPPS PLAZA
Belford Shoumate, architect
1940

Each of the two side wings of this house terminates in a small pavilion. The house and pavilions have Bermuda concrete tile roofs. Windows and doors are either rectangular or arched with louvered shutters.

226 and 228 PHIPPS PLAZA
Howard Major, architect
1939

A screened verandah with a Chinese balustrade stretches across the front of number 226, a tropical cottage. The entrance lintel also denotes a Chinese influence. The walls are sheathed in horizontal wooden boards. The asphalt shingle hipped roof extends over the verandah. The house at 228 Phipps Plaza is a one story wood structure with a hipped roof with asphalt tiles, sliding sash windows, and French doors. A screened porch along the front has a decorative wood balustrade.

232, 233, 234, 235, 236, 238
PHIPPS PLAZA
Marion S. Wyeth, architect of 232, 236, 238
Maurice Fatio, architect of 234
1927

These office and commercial units abut the sidewalk and display a wide variety of Spanish details. Recessed doorways are protected by ornate iron gates with accompanying brackets and lanterns. Heavy wood brackets and columns with chamfered corners are in the Southwestern Spanish tradition. One ground story window has a ceramic tile moulding. The garden and building walls are troweled stucco, creating a homogenous surface texture. Behind the walls are private gardens.

SOUTHWEST COMMERCIAL
CORNER
264 South County Road
Addison Mizner, architect
1930

The massive scale of the rusticated entrance piers and the underscaling of the windows on the side elevation make the building appear quite large. The entire building is sheathed in cut coral stone, creating a richly textured surface which is enhanced by the decorated entrance, the Renaissance cornice, and the various mouldings.

NORTHWEST COMMERCIAL
CORNER
Harvey and Clarke, architects
270-280 South County Road
1920s

One building of seven units and another building of three bays comprise this commercial unit. The units of the large building are separated by pilasters with intricate designs which also elaborate the entrances. Every other unit on the second story has a cast iron balcony. The window patterns are in the same order on both sides of the center balcony, thus unifying the design. The separate building displays much simpler details.

The windows of the smaller building are framed by various sized stone block veneers. The center ground story windows are shaded by a wood canopy with elaborate carved patterns. A most interesting feature is the small built-in bench completely covered with Spanish ceramic tiles.

FOUR ARTS LIBRARY
Four Arts Plaza
Maurice Fatio, architect
1936
additions, Marion S. Wyeth, 1946

This Quattrocento style building has simple cast stone features: columns, moldings, lintels, the belt course and the balustrade. The three-bay entrance loggia is decorated with murals on canvas and it has a cut coral stone floor.

SINGER OFFICE BUILDING
and EMBASSY APARTMENTS
441-437 Royal Palm Way
Addison Mizner, architect
1925
alterations, John Volk, 1947

Originally the ground story had full-length Gothic windows. After the alteration of the ground story, this building appears as an essentially modern structure with only traces of historic stylistic borrowings. The base of the building is scored stucco, simulating rusticated masonry blocks. The fascia, between the first and second stories, is decorated with heraldic designs. The numerous balconies vary in depth and length but they all have simple iron balustrades and some have simple curvilinear brackets.

EMBASSY-FOUR ARTS BUILDING
455 Royal Palm Way
Addison Mizner and Lester Geisler, architects
1928
conversion, John Volk, 1947

The asymmetrical placement of decorative details distinguishes this building. The projecting entrance wall displays an uneven disposition of pilasters crowned with finials. The entire upper section of the entrance wall is cut coral stone. On either side of the arched wooden doorway are ornate iron lanterns. The windows display a variety of forms: rectangular and segmental arched on the ground story, and circular and octagonal on the upper stories.

294-296 HIBISCUS AVENUE
Maurice Fatio, architect
1920s

The classical elements on this urban house are executed in cut coral stone. The columns, mouldings and window sills are formed from this indigenous material. Wrought iron was used for the balcony balustrade and the ornamental supporting brackets. The exposed decorated roof rafters are visible on the eaves. The outer stair wall displays the profile of the steps.

MIZNER FOUNTAIN
AND MEMORIAL PARK
South County Road
Addison Mizner, architect
1929

The Park extends down the middle of South County Road. It consists of a long narrow reflecting pool flanked by trimmed shrubs and a cut coral stone pavement. Side alleys of flowers and palm trees border the walkway that leads to the fountain plaza. At the four corners of the plaza are cut coral stone piers with attached basins, animal heads, and urns. The stucco fountain is made up of horses and three basins.

204 BRAZILIAN AVENUE
(OLD DAILY NEWS BUILDING)
Harvey and Clarke, architects
1927
addition, Addison Mizner, 1927-1928

Occupying a prominent corner in the Town Hall Square
Historic District, this building was the original location of
the offices of the Palm Beach *Daily News*. Designed as a
straightforward commercial building, this is a less elaborate design than other Harvey and Clark buildings on the
Town Hall Square, such as 365 South County Road and the
Town Hall. The main decoration is found in cast-stone
pilasters with a vine motif. These pilasters were a stock architectural element found on many Harvey and Clarke buildings of the period. This building is listed on the National
Register of Historic Places.

BRAZILIAN COURT HOTEL
310 Brazilian Avenue
Rosario Candela, architect
1920s
additions, Maurice Fatio

Its simplicity emphasized by the slender, tall Royal Palms
that border it, the Brazilian Court Hotel has three stories
except for an open deck area, corner balconies, and blind
arches above the second floor fenestration. From the
entrance walk, one sees a series of barrel tile roofs over various one story wings. Ornamented iron grilles protect the
first story windows along the walk. A fine inner courtyard
is charmingly landscaped.

345 BRAZILIAN AVENUE
Early Twentieth Century

Tapered square piers, an open porch, a dormer window, and a broad overhanging gable roof mark this early house as a typical Palm Beach bungalow. This example is relatively unaltered and retains its original shingle walls.

141 AUSTRALIAN AVENUE
Early Twentieth Century

This house is a somewhat simple version of the Shingle Style, popular at the turn of the century. It consists of a gabled structure with side dormers and a one story front wing of two rooms. A gabled roof covers one room and extends over the deeply recessed front door. Half a hipped roof covers the other room. As its style suggests, the house is completely covered with wooden shingles.

159 AUSTRALIAN AVENUE
Early Twentieth Century

The pitched roof of this one and a half story house extends well beyond the walls of the house forming the roof to the verandah. The four bay dormer which, like the house, has deep eaves, is exceptionally large. Both the verandah and dormer eaves have exposed rafters and braces. The verandah arches are stucco as is the chimney.

CITY HALL AND FIRE STATION
360 South County Road
Harvey and Clarke, architects
1926
restoration, Jeffrey Smith, 1989

This is a textured stucco building that is eclectic in both form and details, drawing upon classical, Romanesque and Renaissance sources. The windows are all coupled: rectangular on the ground story and arched on the second story. The ground story apsidal wing has Mediterranean arcades. Between the windows and arcades are engaged Corinthian columns. The capital motif is repeated on the second story corner window impost blocks. Classical patera decorate the balconies and the Romanesque tower. This photo shows the building before restoration.

COMMERCIAL CORNER
365 South County Road
Harvey and Clarke, architects
1926

An arcade of round arches with Tuscan columns on pedestals surrounds this two story commercial building. The underscaling of the classical details —the arcade, the urns, and finials—makes the building appear larger than it is. A cast iron balustrade replaces the parapet where the arcade turns the corner. A variety of fenestration and mouldings occurs on the second story. One elevation of the taller corner block has a statue in a niche in the manner of the Mission style.

141 CHILEAN AVENUE
ca. 1910

The heavy porch piers of oolite, a form of limestone, are typical of Florida bungalows in the early period. The two story element in the rear is somewhat unusual in the Bungaloid style, which is more frequently one and one half stories; however, the broad roof overhang and exposed rafter ends are both characteristic of the style. Wood shingles are also often found on Florida bungalows.

150 CHILEAN AVENUE
Charles Snyder, architect
1929

This heavily Moorish-influenced house was constructed as the residence of the architect. It is notable for its elaborate meshrebeeyeh with cinquefoil-arched windows projecting over a lattice door and its slender minaret decorated with Arabic script in low relief. A pointed arch defines the driveway and trefoil arched windows decorate the side facade. The two-story apartment with garage in the rear has its own small minaret.

230 CHILEAN AVENUE
Early Twentieth Century

The Bungaloid and International Styles influenced the design of this house. The massive tapered porch piers suggest those commonly found on the bungalows in California and the northern states.

The cubic volume of the house is emphasized by the relatively flat roofs with wide projecting eaves, the rectangular windows, and the lack of ornamentation.

The strong horizontal emphasis of the roofs and the simplicity of form are characteristics of the International Style, an early modern architectural development in opposition to nineteenth century eclecticism.

234 CHILEAN AVENUE
Early Twentieth Century

This two story, stucco house is an adaptation of the Bungaloid and Western Stick styles that developed in California. Although the true bungalow is only one story, the broad roofs with wide eaves and the heavy tapered porch piers are common features of the style. The exposed wood framing of the porte cochere and the strong horizontal emphasis of the projecting roofs express the influence of modern Californian architectural developments. The hipped roofs are covered with asbestos paper.

325 CHILEAN AVENUE
Addison Mizner, architect
1925

Mizner's only two-unit design in Palm Beach is still occupied by its original owner. The side facade shows a pleasing variety of Mediterranean Revival details such as pecky cypress at the window heads and roof eaves, and the corbeled window treatment on the upper story.

317 PERUVIAN AVENUE
Early Twentieth Century

This house with the subtle ornamentation is early twentieth century modern. The strong horizontality of the projecting roofs supplies built-in shade for the structure. The predominant modern influence is that of the Stick Style as evident by the exposed framing on the porte cochere and the rectangular patterns on the screened porch and above, between the second story windows. This ornamentation also suggests the influence of designs by Frank Lloyd Wright.

341 PERUVIAN AVENUE
Marion S. Wyeth, architect
1930

The Gothic window mouldings, balconies, and the cylindrical brick chimney are derivatives of Venetian architectural forms. The surface sculpture and mouldings are of cast stone. Cut coral stone was utilized for the capping on the piers of the garden gate adjacent to the house. On the top is a small sculpture of the lion of St. Mark. At the entrance to the property there is a Spanish Romanesque archway with brick arches and an iron gate. Engaged columns adorn the piers. Like the house the entrance wall has a barrel tile roof. The house has a fine garden with an elaborate cascading fountain.

MAJOR ALLEY
411-417 Major Alley
Howard Major, architect
1925

Like Addison Mizner, Howard Major designed an alley in Bermudian style which he named after himself. It is a most significant development because of the amount of liveable space created on such a small piece of land. The architect imaginatively built up the entire property with many charming houses. Zoning codes no longer permit the total utilization of a property for a building.

The one-and-a-half and two-story houses are cement base stucco with a heavy application of lime stucco to create rounded edges. The windows and doors on the street levels have louvered shutters and the second story balconies are completely louvered. Several entrances and balconies have lattice trim.

363 COCOANUT ROW
1925
alterations, John Volk, 1937
alterations, Ray Plockelman,1960

A tower with round headed arches, a parapet with swagged cartouche, and deeply recessed two story openings with flattened arches form the major ornament of this rather ordinary Mediterranean Revival design. A belt course and balconies delineate the upper stories. The building is constructed around an entrance courtyard, and has been in use as a hotel from early days. This building is listed on the National Register of Historic Places.

353-333 WORTH AVENUE
Addison Mizner, architect
1924

Contrived and telescoped history was a Mizner device for creating a picturesque composition. This stretch of Worth Avenue was built as a single design, though it suggests a number of private undertakings. Classical, Gothic, Renaissance, and Spanish Creole elements interact throughout the buildings. Dominating the whole, tower-like, is Mizner's own house. Two shopping alleys, Via Mizner and Via Parigi, are incorporated into the complex.

236, 240½, 244½, 246, 246½
WORTH AVENUE
Howard Major, architect
1930

A most sedate building by an architect well versed in eclecticism. The simple, two story structure has a slightly projecting center gable. The larger second story window units have slender, simple engaged columns. Part of the ground story has been altered but some of the original arched entrances are still evident.

250, 256-260, 262-264, 266-310, 312
WORTH AVENUE
Maurice Fatio, architect
1920s

This complex structure contains both commercial and residential units. It varies in height from two to four stories and has an interior courtyard with a garden and a fountain. Cut coral stone and stucco mouldings, cornices, columns, and balustrades articulate the structure.

The large window and door arches are round and lancet, some with trefoil cusps.

A variety of simple and ornate ironwork adorn the balconies and exterior stairs.

EVERGLADES CLUB
356 Worth Avenue
Addison Mizner, architect
1918

This is Mizner's first Florida building, the result of a conversation with Paris Singer at a time when both men thought they were dying and were looking for diversion. Intended as a convalescent home for war veterans, it emerged as a club, most exclusive, and made Singer for a number of years the social dictator of Palm Beach. Venetian Gothic windows, a bell tower in the manner of a California Spanish mission church, latticed balconies of Moorish extraction, an imaginative use of colored tiles in a variety of places, and an arcade with tiled spandrels —also Moorish—are combined through the mediation of tinted stucco, barrel-tiled roofs, and striped awnings. Inside are raftered ceilings and stucco walls, with wrought-iron and leaded-glass lighting fixtures. In the dining room above the walnut paneling, is an artfully antiqued mural by Achille Angeli.

450 WORTH AVENUE
Addison Mizner, architect
1921

This is a most unique house in that it rises from the water. The house is accessible by both land and "sea." The land entrance has a quarry key walk that leads to an elaborate arch doorway with a low relief sculpture of the Lion of St. Mark above a partially paneled oak door. The "sea" entrance consists of a Venetian boat entrance with a balustraded boat landing. The second story windows have numerous balconies which overlook the water. The large chimney is cantilevered on brackets and has a dovecote.

12 GOLFVIEW ROAD
Marion S. Wyeth, architect
1922

Spanish and Venetian motifs accent this house. Before a recent renovation the frequent use of Spanish ceramic tiles was visible along the exterior stepped wall of the entrance and side stairs. The stair that ascends from the ground level to the roof was completely covered by ceramic tiles. The Venetian balconies are cast stone and the corresponding ogee arches and cable moulding above the windows are stucco. The house is partially screened from view by a half story wall with an ornate iron gate.

15 GOLFVIEW ROAD
Marion S. Wyeth, architect
1921

This house is L-shaped in plan with an interior courtyard. The main body of the house has an elaborate, cor-
belled brick cornice. The various arch window forms have
cast stone mouldings. In relation to the house, the entrance
wing is a humble structure and suggests medieval
origins. The cut coral stone blocks with an elaborate
heraldic decoration surround the segmental arch entrance.
Recessed within this arch is an iron door with an intricate pattern; the iron grille work on the small side windows
is much simpler. The entry pavement is brick laid in
herringbone pattern.

16 GOLFVIEW ROAD
Marion S. Wyeth, architect
1924

The entrance tower is a prominent and popular feature on many Palm Beach houses. Here the massive Spanish tower is lavishly adorned with low-relief sculptural motifs that recall Antiquity and Renaissance. Classical festoons, obelisks, heraldic shields, and richly carved panels embellish the entrance and window mouldings. Above the casement windows are cypress wood lintels, and the third-story window arcades are in the form of segmental arches. The textured stucco enlivens the wall surfaces.

17 GOLFVIEW ROAD
Marion S. Wyeth, architect
1921

This low, rambling complex terminates in a four-story tower. The profile of the curved bell cap moulding of the tower recalls the Spanish Mission style. Throughout the structure the Spanish tile moulding panels and the iron grillework blend easily with the Renaissance arches and balustrades.

19 GOLFVIEW ROAD
Maurice Fatio, architect
Late 1920s

This simple Louisiana style house was built during the reaction against the Mediterranean picturesque styles of the 1920s. It has wood board siding and louvered shutters. The dominant features are the arch entrance and the full second story porch with lattice side walls.

598 SOUTH COUNTY ROAD
John Volk, architect
1935

This was the first Bermuda style house built in Palm Beach by John Volk. The architect built the house for himself. This style became fashionable in the late 1920s and early 1930s as the Spanish and Renaissance extravaganzas diminished in popularity. The house is symmetrical in plan with the living quarters located a half story below the entrance. The door, sidelights, and porch walls all have louvers. Louvers are a useful architectural element for this semi-tropical climate as they not only give privacy but let air and light in while keeping the heavy afternoon rains out. Above the entrance is a semi-elliptical fanlight. The rectangular windows have an abstracted Classical keystone design. The heavy gate piers and the flared central staircase add formality to the small simple house.

5 MIDDLE ROAD
Wyeth and King, architects
1937

A British Colonial work with hipped roofs, bay windows, and a broken pediment surrounding the entrance portico, this house retains some of its original interior wallpaper. The symetrical main facade has a recessed central element flanked by projecting blocks. Quoining defines the corners of the wings. The house projects a particularly refined and balanced character.

25 MIDDLE ROAD
1926

On either side of the arched doorway are coupled corkscrew columns with ornate capitals. Between the columns are concave niches. Behind the decorative semi-circular iron gate is a carved paneled double door; above it is a most elaborate iron and glass light. The narrow entrance lintel and the iron balustrade form a small balcony on the second story. The window above has a heavy flat moulding and a Spanish iron grille. The desire for decoration was extended to the vents which display an ornate silhouette.

61 MIDDLE ROAD
Marion S. Wyeth, architect
1924

This Mediterranean Revival house was constructed as the architect's own home. The relatively restrained facade focuses on the entrance, which is surmounted by a decorative cartouche. The house is constructed around a central courtyard and is organized around its three interior fountains and the open spaces surrounding them, hence the name given the house by the architect and owner, "Tres Fontanes." Marion S. Wyeth designed a number of distinguished buildings on Middle Road.

550 SOUTH OCEAN BOULEVARD
Maurice Fatio, architect
1930

The three story entrance block of this house is faced in quarry key, which creates a strong contrast in color and texture to the smooth stucco walls of the rest of the house. This facing material is repeated on the window mouldings, cornices and decorative bands throughout the structure. The numerous variations of the arch motif and the ironwork add further decorative qualities to this house.

79 MIDDLE ROAD
Maurice Fatio, architect
1927

Because of the massive belvedere, this house acquires a truly large appearance. The arched windows are recessed between cast stone piers and the coupled rectangular windows are framed in wood. The recessed oak door is in the shape of an ogee arch. The cast stone cornice on the belvedere displays a triangular pattern.

On the interior is a magnificently landscaped courtyard enclosed by loggias.

91 MIDDLE ROAD
Addison Mizner, architect
1922-23
additions, Wyeth, King, and Johnson, 1954, 1962

The entrance consists of a Palladian motif with paired
Ionic columns. Round arched and rectangular windows
are used on the west facade. The east facade is marked by
a prominent central block and decorative trefoil windows.
The 1954 alterations changed the main entrance of the
house from Ocean Boulevard to Middle Road.

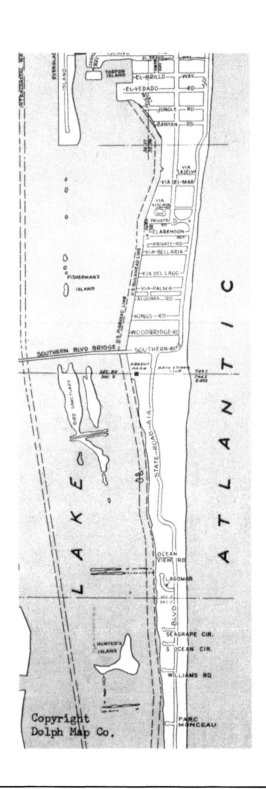

EL BRAVO WAY
AND SOUTH

4 EL BRAVO WAY
Marion S. Wyeth, architect
1920
alterations, Addison Mizner, 1927

This house was originally built in the Italian Renaissance tradition, but the later alterations and the additions of the cast stone battlements and heavy window mouldings have transformed the structure into a feudal fantasy. The heavy wooden door with decorative iron studs promotes the medieval appearance. The slender columns between the windows, the lintel where the door previously existed, and the wall heraldry are remnants from the original construction.

100 EL BRAVO WAY
Marion S. Wyeth, architect
1923
alterations, Howard Major, 1928

The absolute simplicity of this house emphasizes the very subtle details. On the ground story, the upper panes of glass have curved corners. The iron balustrades consist of twisted rods and the window grilles have a subdued design. The recessed arched entrance is the only departure from the rectangularity of the structure. The glazed wall niche is a unique feature, while a column between one of the second story windows is a prevalent decorative motif.

220 EL BRAVO WAY
Volk and Maass, architects
1927

Similar to an even more elaborate Volk and Maass design
at 252 El Bravo Way, this house is notable for the fanciful
use of brick in its tower, which seems to perch uneasily on
open arches. Modern windows have been inserted in
many places, but the panel of cinquefoil-arched windows
on the front facade is still a strong decorative element.
The outstanding iron door has a pair of dragons in its
round headed arch. An elaborate design of cast stone
columns and cast plaster decoration further emphasizes
the doorway.

252 EL BRAVO WAY
Volk and Maass, architects
1928

The two-story Spanish Renaissance entrance intensifies the complexity of this irregularly massed structure. The large cusped arch window has Gothic origins and the iron balustrade is in the Spanish tradition. The elaborate cast-stone mouldings and balustrade are well-scaled to the size of the house. The smooth stucco wall creates an excellent background for the lavish details.

237 EL BRAVO WAY
Julius Jacobs, architect
1924

The U-plan of this house creates a small entrance court-yard. The wall with its iron gate protects it from view. Several windows have iron grilles with crestings similar to that of the gate. The center section of the house consists of three French doors with arch lights. The entire second floor is a wall of casement windows with classical attached columns and a cyprus wood lintel. The classical column motif is repeated on the recessed porch to one side of the courtyard and on the exterior porch of one of the wings.

343 EL BRAVO WAY
Volk and Maass, architects
1930

The bold entrance to the motor courtyard resembles a classical triumphal arch. The smooth stucco surface of the walls emphasize the silhouette and texture of the cast stone moulding while the intricate ironwork of the lanterns, window grilles, and dome over the courtyard well contrast with the severity of the remainder of the structure. The courtyard contains a charming stone and iron well head.

300 EL BRILLO WAY
Maurice Fatio, architect
1936

The white mottled brick gives an antique appearance to this Louisiana style house. The second story verandah is constructed of wood with exposed floor joists. Above the windows are splayed brick flat arches. Recessed within a series of brick arches is the door with a simple fanlight.

100 EL BRILLO WAY
Addison Mizner, architect
1924
additions, Marion S. Wyeth

This is a simple two story house with a barrel tile roof; it has an arched cast stone entranceway and a wrought iron gate. Two arched windows are located over the entrance and the larger window to the right has a shallow ogee molding.

101 EL BRILLO WAY
1921
Marion S. Wyeth, architect
addition, Marion S. Wyeth, 1922

The main section of this house consists of three parts; a low two story wing with paired casement windows above and three arched windows below, a center section with arched doorway and French windows facing a balcony above, and a taller section with a large arched Georgian casement window and cast stone cartouche above. This wing also has stucco quoins at the corners. There is a variety of ornamental iron at both the first and second floor levels.

134 EL VEDADO
John Volk, architect
1935

Probably the most unusual architectural style in Palm
Beach is the half-timber Norman house form as such
houses were originally found in cold northern climates.
Here the ground story is brick that has been painted off
white. At the corners the brick is laid in a diagonal pattern.
Wood framing forms the entrance porch, and the second
floor is half-timber and stucco. The casement windows and
the shutters are built of wood. The terra cotta tile hipped
roof has a subtly flared profile.

137 EL VEDADO
1926

Built around an open courtyard, this house assumes the form of a Mediterranean farmhouse. Decorative panels of cast stone, the windows and a fanciful iron gate add elaboration.

200 EL VEDADO
Maurice Fatio, architect
1939
additions, Simonson and Walling, 1945

This simple frame structure is enlivened by the upward curved rafters and the Oriental carved planks along the gable ends of the house. The pitched roof is of cypress wood shakes. At the corners are attached square columns. The canopy above the door repeats the exotic flared profile of the roof.

319 EL VEDADO
Clarence Mack, architect
1930

Restraint and control dominate this Neo-Classical design. Late Georgian stylistic elements are present in the projecting central bay emphasized by Ionic pilasters, the repetition of the roof pediment over the lower windows, and the rusticated lower story.

684 PELICAN LANE
John Volk, architect
1938

A balanced Bermuda style residence with two wings
flanking a taller center element. Dormer windows are
used in the side wings. The doorway is emphasized with
a round arch. A simple fence adds definition to the entrance
court.

105 JUNGLE ROAD
Marion S. Wyeth, architect
1924

The juxtaposition of the three story tower and the one and two story wings creates a dramatic composition. The two story entrance details recall the High Renaissance, but the form of the house with the window arcades and cloisters is Romanesque. The Spanish-Moorish influence is evident by the window grilles and the incised scroll design on the panels on the tower.

102 JUNGLE ROAD
Addison Mizner, architect
1921
alterations, Maurice Fatio; Wyeth, King, and Johnson;
John Volk

The four most important Palm Beach architects of the
1920s worked on this house at various times. The stucco
masses of the house are embellished with stone and brick
window lintels and sills. The balconies have intricate
curvilinear iron balustrades. A large wooden bay
window section projects from the main block of the house.
Many of the windows as well as the shutters
are louvered.

240 BANYAN ROAD
1929

Because this house has little ornamentation, the Italian Renaissance entrance is most pronounced. The heavy rustication of the cast stone columns is in strong contrast to the textured stucco walls. The entrance extends two stories incorporating an elaborate cornice with obelisks and a decorative window embellished with a richly carved moulding and an iron grille. The arched door is recessed within this frame. The diamond pattern window and the iron balcony are the only other decorations. Originally there was a large tower which would have balanced the scale of the entrance to the house.

This house was demolished before this book reached the printer.

235 BANYAN ROAD
Howard Major, architect
1925

The rusticated cast stone arch, a Florentine architectural motif, is the predominant feature on this Spanish style house. The iron gate recessed within the arch is in the Spanish-Moorish tradition. The smooth stucco wall accentuates the color and texture of this ornate entrance. In addition to the iron window grilles, a wrought iron lantern and an iron wheel of bells are on the entrance wall.

209 BANYAN ROAD
Maurice Fatio, architect
1934

This Louisiana style house displays a Romanesque arched entrance. Recessed within the series of arches is a wooden panel and bolt door. The brick house is painted white with the exception of the bricks under the roof line which are left in their original tones. The windows have brick flat arches and paneled shutters. Underneath the second story balcony the floor joists that join the columns are more pronounced than the adjacent ones.

196 BANYAN ROAD
Volk and Maass, architects
1929

The entrance way in the Spanish Romanesque tradition is the dominant feature of the house. The stone facing encompasses the second story window and balcony; the wooden paneled double door is recessed within the elaborately carved arches of the portal. In sharp contrast to the heavy moulding around the stone entrance is the delicate iron work of the balcony balustrade and the window grilles. However, the use of stone is repeated throughout the structure for the cornice and window lintels and sills.

133 BANYAN ROAD
Julius Jacobs, architect
1927

A variety of bold architectural elements and subtle details adorn this structure. The decorative Spanish tile entrance surrounds an ornate iron gate behind which is the front door and a rope moulding surrounds the tiles. Leaded glass panels form the rectangular ground story windows. They are separated by square wooden columns. Below are recessed squared panels with the stepped pattern of the entranceway. The large arch windows are treated in a classical manner with projecting sills, and are protected by Spanish grilles. The cornice has a brick saw-tooth pattern above the exposed decorative rafters. The arcaded belvedere has a flared roof and recessed panels with an incised scroll design. The wing perpendicular to the entrance has an elaborate cast stone Gothic balustrade.

710 SOUTH OCEAN BOULEVARD
Mrs. Alfred Kay, architect
1920s

Several noteworthy features are incorporated into the
design of this house. Spanning the entrance drive is an
open-air bridge with a pitched roof. A Romanesque-style
arcaded porch forms the south entry to the house. The
courtyard wall is broken by a small projecting entrance with
a wooden, lathe turned gate and an iron grille forms a
cage over one of the south windows.

720 SOUTH OCEAN BOULEVARD
Addison Mizner, architect
1919
addition, Maurice Fatio

This house acquires its character from restraint of ornamentation and the generous endowment of window area.
The south pavilion has arched windows of leaded stained
glass. Above the second story balcony is a row of casement
windows with a cypress wood lintel. Recessed within the
wall arcades are casement windows with semi-circular
fanlights. The windows are separated by attached columns.
Chimneys are capped with barrel tiles, and the wall around
the house has classical motifs. The architect built this
house for himself.

750 SOUTH COUNTY ROAD
Belford Shoumate, architect
1941

The raised first floor and pedimented entrance are typical Bermudian features in this restrained design.

754 SOUTH COUNTY ROAD
Benjamin Hoffman, architect
1923

The tower with arch windows give to this house an ecclesiastical appearance. It indeed does have an interior cloister. The arch windows are slightly recessed, only the arched entrance has a moulding. In contrast are the classical pediment, cornice and incised pilasters on the main part of the house.

780 SOUTH OCEAN BOULEVARD
Addison Mizner, architect
1925

This Italian house has Venetian horseshoe cusped arches with leaded glass windows. Two features that have become trademarks of architect Addison Mizner are the Venetian chimney piece that begins on the second floor, and the exterior staircase. The latter in this case, was a necessary addition to the original plans when it was realized the interior stairs were accidentally omitted from the plans. The windows from section to section are at different levels creating an irregular surface pattern. The numerous Renaissance features include the attached columns, the balustrades, and the extensive gardens with an elaborate fountain and pool.

790 SOUTH COUNTY ROAD
Maurice Fatio, architect
1934

This simple Spanish style building has a large balcony with a cut stone moulding. The balconies and windows have iron grillework, and louvered French doors open onto the balconies. The property is entered through rusticated stone piers with an elaborate iron gate. This building was the garage and servant complex for the house across the County Road. The structure as pictured is undergoing restoration and construction of a large addition.

115 VIA LA SELVA
Maurice Fatio, architect
1928

The rustication of a Tuscan entrance is repeated in the heavy quoining at the corners of this Mediterranean Revival residence. The use of arched and rectangular windows adds variety.

801 SOUTH COUNTY ROAD
Maurice Fatio, architect
1930

The open groined vault entranceway that penetrates the rectangular house block creates an effective solid-void composition. The extensive use of cut coral stone is evident on the entrance columns, on the picture window lintel and moulding, and on the second story balcony.

800 SOUTH COUNTY ROAD
Addison Mizner, architect
1923
addition, Addison Mizner, 1926

The two wings of the large house are divided by a canal that runs in a north-south direction, and an overpass with an arched roof connects the wings. Originally the house was directly on the shore line but later land was filled in. The house has an extensive window area and numerous cast stone balconies. On the lake side are French doors that open onto a terrace. The stucco reveals a roughly trowelled texture.

821 SOUTH COUNTY ROAD
Maurice Fatio, architect
1928

This Italian Romanesque house is entirely faced and trimmed with cut coral stone. The cornice arcade is filled with horizontal and herringbone brick patterns. The elaborate carved entrance and window mouldings recall Florentine motifs. In contrast to the heavy wooden panel-and-bolt double door are the light delicate window grilles. The balconies, on the ocean side, are of cast stone. In the cloistered courtyard is a cut coral stone fountain.

822 SOUTH COUNTY ROAD
Maurice Fatio, architect
1937
alterations, Marion S. Wyeth, 1963

The Georgian house has been continually revived from the late nineteenth century onward. Here the brick walls are laid in a roughly textured Flemish bond. There are brick quoins, a belt course between the first and second stories, and splayed brick flat arches above the windows. The brick is nineteenth century and was used as ballast in English ships traveling outward to the Grenadines and returning with a cargo of spices.

The slightly projecting pedimented center bay has a semicircular portico with slender fluted columns. The fanlight above the door consists of one pane of glass. On either side of the entrance and on the pediment are *oeils-de-boeuf* windows. A thin iron balustrade tops the portico.

204 VIA DEL MAR
Maurice Fatio, architect
1920s

Simple in form and detail, this house nevertheless displays a heavy entrance and balcony. A paneled door is recessed within the coral frame and the iron balustrade above creates a small balcony from the entrance lintel. The cornice consists of a double scalloped border which repeats the profile of the pantile roof above.

210 VIA DEL MAR
Maurice Fatio, architect
1928

The Norman half-timber house developed in a cold, north-ern climate and is therefore unusual as a stylistic proto-type for a Southern dwelling. Here the ground story is brick painted white with wood trim. The projecting sec-ond story is half-timber with stucco. The steeply hipped roof is covered with flat terra cotta tiles, and the tall brick chimney is red brick mottled with white paint.

840 SOUTH OCEAN BOULEVARD
Marion S. Wyeth, architect
1928

The arch entranceway is the focal point on the central portion of this house. The paneled double door is recessed in the arch of cut coral stone voussoirs. On either side are elaborate iron filigree lanterns. Cut coral is also used on the horizontal bands under windows and for the columns between the three center windows on the second story. Above these windows is a cypress wood lintel. The house is symmetrical in plan and has Bermuda style louvered shutters.

850 SOUTH OCEAN BOULEVARD
Julius Jacobs, architect
1928

The house displays a multitude of two-and-three dimensional surface patterns. The diamond motif of the painted tiles is repeated on the French doors below and suggested by the first floor Gothic window arches. The shaded recesses of the arcade and balcony enhance the light and dark patterns. The textures on the capitals and columns and the shadows cast from the balustrades and brackets further enrich the decorative facade.

860 SOUTH OCEAN BOULEVARD
Julius Jacobs, architect
1929

The entrance composition of this house of carved stone and glazed wrought iron is perhaps the most elaborate in all of Palm Beach. Grotesques and gargoyles are carved on the entrance pilasters, on the brackets. column capitals, and on various corners of the house. A fifteenth century Spanish Gothic moulding forms the cornice of the tower. Part of the structure has a barrel vault pantile roof. The dining room on the ocean front resembles that of a ship's prow and offers a panoramic view of the ocean. The house is equipped with a pipe organ and a carrillon. The swimming pool, which offers one the choice of salt, fresh, or sulphur water, is approached by a cut stone staircase with marble treads.

874 SOUTH COUNTY ROAD
Harvey and Clarke, architects
1923

The interior courtyard is protected from view by the front wall that extends from the main part of the house. The curvilinear profile of the wall recalls the Spanish Mission style. The wooden door with recessed panels and bolts accurately delineates its Spanish origin. In contrast to the solid wall are the arched windows on the gable end of the house. The grille over the windows, the classical engaged columns between the windows, and the textured stucco create a picturesque composition.

181 LAKE PARK DRIVE
Marion S. Wyeth, architect
ca. 1920s

A recently restored example of Marion S. Wyeth's work, this house displays blind trefoil arched and rectangular windows along with trefoil, pointed, and round-arched openings, all on the same facade. The entrance bay is further decorated with a panel of decorative plaster bosses. The Venetian Gothic details of the main building form a contrast to the Tunisian influenced domed pavilion on the south portion of the property.

105 CLARENDON AVENUE
Marion S. Wyeth, architect
1926

This Italian villa house form is simply articulated with Classical motifs. The pedimented center wall sections slightly project from the mass of the house. The rusticated gate piers are capped with carved pineapples, the symbol of hospitality. The arched entrance is emphasized by the bust and scroll sculpture. Above the large ground story windows are projecting lintels while the other windows have simple mouldings or remain unadorned. A Renaissance balcony with ornamental bracket supports, and recessed wall panels depicting classical festoon carvings adorn the terrace elevation.

920 SOUTH OCEAN BOULEVARD
Maurice Fatio, architect
1928

This Italian Romanesque house form is entirely constructed of cut coral stone with alternating horizontal
bands of brick. The lavish, intricate carvings on the surfaces are stone, and ironwork painted to resemble stone.
The entrance is one of the most ornate doorways in Palm
Beach. The walkway leading to it is brick laid in a herringbone pattern with quarry key edging. Ornamental
iron is also used for some of the doors, balustrades, window grilles and the entrance lanterns. The casement windows and French doors are recessed within arches or
rectangular mouldings. The numerous, large chimneys
are unusual for the climate but they are perfectly pro-
portioned to the large scale of the house.

930 SOUTH OCEAN BOULEVARD
Maurice Fatio, architect
1928

This is a most uncommon structure as it is entirely sheathed in cut coral stone. Herringbone brick patterns enhance the textured coral surface. The arcades with slender columns, decorative iron window and balcony grilles and cast stone brackets embellish this Romanesque style house. The low hipped roof is of barrel tiles . The arch windows and the arcades create a fluent rhythmic movement along the ground story.

150 VIA BELLARIA
Maurice Fatio, architect
1927

The Quattrocento Tuscan Villa house form is enriched by the Spanish-Moorish grillework and the decorative features on the cornice. The elaborate entrance consists of an arch or irregular stone voussoirs that surround the recessed paneled wooden door. Above the door is a carved shell motif—a favorite Spanish ornament. Like the door, the rectangular and arched casement windows are surrounded by stone mouldings. Barrel tiles form the low hipped roof. Several interior courtyards continue the irregular style and form of the house's Mediterranean heritage.

125 VIA DEL LAGO
Marion S. Wyeth, architect
1929

The Tuscan entrance is surmounted by a balcony with turned wood balusters. The low hipped roof is set off by decorative brickwork under the eaves. Painted shutters enhance the effect of the windows. The double entrance steps are a modern addition.

174 VIA DEL LAGO
Marion S. Wyeth, architect
1933

This Louisiana style house has delicate details most evident in the balcony iron work which is painted white to blend with the white stucco. The formal, Adamesque entrance consists of a fanlight, sidelights, and a balustrade and railing which echo more simply the iron patterns from the balcony.

MAR-A-LAGO
1100 South Ocean Boulevard
Joseph Urban; Marion S. Wyeth, architects
1924-1927

In 1972 Mar-a-Lago was placed on the National Register, the official list of historical structures and sites, as a
National Historic Landmark. The National Register is
maintained by the Department of the Interior. The building has been fully documented by the Historic American Buildings Survey.

Joseph Urban, one of the designers of the house, was also
the designer of the Ziegfeld Theater in New York and
numerous other Art Deco buildings. The result is that
Mar-a-Lago is undoubtedly the most sumptuous residence in Palm Beach. The main two story section ram-
bles on into a series of one story wings. The horizontal
mass is dramatically offset by the massive belvedere and
the numerous fanciful chimneys. The abundance of elaborate cast stone and plaster wall patterns, the Spanish
ceramic tiles, and lathe-turned and beaded grilles create
a unique, outstanding structure. The detail work throughout this house is truly magnificent.

BATH AND TENNIS CLUB
1170 South Ocean Boulevard
Joseph Urban, architect
1926
additions, Marion S. Wyeth, 1926
additions, John Volk, 1948

This large rambling structure incorporates Spanish elements in both plan and ornamentation. The plan consists of numerous small courtyards, lounges, reading and card rooms, and a large swimming pool court enclosed by loggias. The large crescent shaped living room opens onto a loggia. The terrace, now enclosed, runs the full length of the living room and incorporates the original five full length arch windows. Cast stone columns and capitals with solid brackets above adorn the courts and loggias. On the interior, there is cypress paneling, iron and leaded chandeliers, exposed ceiling rafters with antique brushed finishes, and quarry tile and basket weave brick lacquered floors. There are two Renaissance fireplaces in the living room.

1200 SOUTH OCEAN BOULEVARD
Addison Mizner, architect
1920

From certain points of view the enormous size of this house is disguised by its echelon plan. Like the California Spanish style it has numerous balconies. On the main sections of the house the ground story windows are arched; the second story windows are rectangular interspersed with small coupled arch windows. The house has hipped and shed barrel tile roofs. All the chimneys have various forms of wind caps.

1300 SOUTH OCEAN BOULEVARD
Abram Garfield, architect
1919
additions, Marion S. Wyeth

From the water this house is broad and rectangular with
a variety of stone mouldings and cast iron details. Viewed
from the road the house is arranged in complex masses that
vary in height from one to five stories. The back of the
house is adorned with elaborate details in the forms of
ornate cornices, lathe-turned cypress wood columns and
balustrades that decorate numerous balconies, ceramic
tiles, and sculptural lintels. The house possesses a number of tall chimneys with a variety of wind caps.

1410 SOUTH OCEAN BOULEVARD
Marion S. Wyeth, architect
1926

The main section of this house is simply a rectangular mass with a pitched roof and a gable end chimney that has a wind cap. The large projecting bay has a hipped roof. The expansive ground story fenestration lightens the effect of this Spanish-style house. The house has paneled wooden shutters and a richly textured stucco surface. The second story window sills that form one sill for two windows are unusual features. The house has been recently remodeled.

1500 SOUTH OCEAN BOULEVARD
Maurice Fatio, architect
1930

The symmetrical plan and details of this imposing house show the influence of Italian Renaissance prototypes. On the second floor, recessed within arches are three sets of French doors that open onto a balcony with a classical Renaissance balustrade. Below are windows with broken pediments and Spanish grilles. On the center section, each window has a stone moulding with a keystone.

On the lake side there are several courtyards; one with a fountain, one with a pool; a fine quarry key staircase leads to the sloping lake front lawn.

1768 SOUTH OCEAN BOULEVARD
Maurice Fatio, architect
1930s

The center and side blocks of this Bermuda style house have hipped roofs with tin shingles. The entrance between the blocks is a variation on a classical portico. The stucco is horizontally scored and this motif is repeated on some of the cornices and lintels. On the center block of the house, the cornice has a subtle curvilinear pattern. Louvered shutters are attached to the sides or the tops of the windows. The entire house is painted white creating a volumetric, sculptural composition.

1820 SOUTH OCEAN BOULEVARD
Addison Mizner, Architect
1924

A California Spanish style porch embellishes the back of this Tudor half-timber and stucco house. The ground story of the entire house is coral rubble and the window lintels are stucco. The circular chimneys are Moorish. A glazed iron gate is recessed within the entrance arch. The center section of the house has a pantile hipped roof while the wings are covered with flat terra cotta tiles. The round chimneys with their mushroom caps are extraordinary features.

1860 SOUTH OCEAN BOULEVARD
Maurice Fatio, architect
1937

The plan and details of this house are derived from Jeffersonian classicism. The central pavilion has a flat hipped roof with a projecting pediment that is flush with the wall below. The side wings have pyramidal roofs. The house is built of red brick that has been painted white creating a mottled antique appearance. Numerous classical details are evident, most of which are found on the center section. These include the arch windows, pilasters, the elaborate cornice, and shell motif in the center of the pediment. With the exception of the arched portal, the wings are more simply detailed. All the windows have keystones; and all the mouldings and trim are constructed from wood. The house is situated on ocean to lake property.

1902 SOUTH OCEAN BOULEVARD
1920s?

This remnant of a larger structure shows typical Mediterranean Revival decorative motifs: elaborate iron gates,
Spanish barrel tile roof, arched windows separated by
cast stone columns, pecky cypress rafter ends, and the
use of polychrome tile on the facade.

LITTLE RED SCHOOLHOUSE
2185 South Ocean Boulevard
1886

The first schoolhouse in southeast Florida, this simple wood structure with vertical siding was constructed with community labor and housed ecumenical religious services as well as the one room school. It has been moved several times and was once used as a gardener's shed. It has now found a permanent home under the auspices of the Town in Phipps Ocean Park, where it is again used as a school in the Preservation Foundation's pioneer education school program. With Sea Gull Cottage it shares the distinction of being the earliest Palm Beach building extant.

IN MEMORIAM

395 NORTH COUNTY ROAD

LOTUS COTTAGE

601 NORTH COUNTY ROAD

513 NORTH COUNTY ROAD

WHITE SANDS, SUNSET AVENUE

WHITE SANDS, SUNSET AVENUE

115 ROYAL POINCIANA WAY

147 ROYAL POINCIANA WAY

260 ROYAL POINCIANA WAY

264 ROYAL POINCIANA WAY

BREAKERS COTTAGES

BREAKERS COTTAGES

BREAKERS COTTAGES

1 SOUTH LAKE TRAIL

6 SOUTH LAKE TRAIL

111 ROYAL PALM WAY

240 CHILEAN AVENUE

SHORWINDS HOTEL

SHORWINDS HOTEL

135 HAMMON AVENUE

243

1425 SOUTH OCEAN BOULEVARD

1800 SOUTH OCEAN BOULEVARD

1960 SOUTH OCEAN BOULEVARD

FIGULUS

NATIONAL REGISTER OF HISTORIC PLACES
LISTING IN THE TOWN OF PALM BEACH

PROPERTY	DATE LISTED
Henry Morrison Flagler House Whitehall Way	12/5/72
The Breakers Hotel One South County Road	8/14/73
Paramount Theatre 139 North County Road	12/12/73
Mar-a-Lago 111 South Ocean Blvd.	12/23/80
U.S. (Main) Post Office 95 North County Road	7/21/83
William Gray Warden Residence 125 Seminole Avenue	8/1/84
Old Daily News Building 204 Brazilian Avenue	12/22/85
Old Vineta Hotel (Listed as Palm Court Hotel) 363 Cocoanut Row	8/21/86

This book was set in Palatino type by Mangis & Associates, of Pittsburgh, Pennsylvania. All photographs are by Barbara D. Hoffstot except for those of Lotus Cottage, which were taken by Maxine Banis and those of the new entries, which are by Stephen B. Leek. The maps are courtesy of the Palm Beach Chamber of Commerce. The Third Edition was edited by Walter C. Kidney of the Pittsburgh History & Landmarks Foundation and was designed by Thomas S. Stevenson, Jr., of Landmarks Design Associates and Jean Hodak of Pittsburgh History & Landmarks Foundation. Original title design by Arnold Bank.

CPSIA information can be obtained
at www.ICGtesting.com
Printed in the USA
LVHW082228041121
702494LV00022B/378